She Laughs at the Future

*15 Inspiring Stories to Give You Joy and Peace
About the Future No Matter Your Season*

She Laughs at the Future

Jill Albanys

with Katelyn Silva, Melissa Eiserer, Helen Corban,
Patricia "Patty" Grace Schaad, Audrey Ostoyic,
Shontal LeJune, Renee Kelley, Karen Powers,
Denise LeDoux Leiato, DeAnna Cavenah, Victoria Bennett,
Zeni Pradel, Dawn Anderson, & Lesa Dale

Butterfly Books Publishing

Contents

Foreword

When you've faced the unthinkable and survived... When you've walked through fire and emerged stronger... When you've stumbled in suffocating darkness but found your way to light... When life has dealt you disappointment, devastation, and despair, yet you've gone on to thrive... These are stories of hope. These are the stories that inspire.

Jill Albanys is one of those rare souls who can see us at our lowest, our most vulnerable, our messiest, and still recognize the good within us. She sees not just who we are, but who we are becoming. Jill comes alongside us in our struggles, cheering us toward victory with an unwavering confidence in the power of God working in and through us.

Perhaps it's because she's been there herself. She knows what it's like to hit rock bottom and still hold on. She's walked through suffering, endured loss, and come out on the other side, healed by God's grace. Because of this, she can look to the future with joy and confidence, knowing that whatever comes, God is in control and will see her through.

Time spent with Jill leaves you inspired and uplifted. She is my friend, my cousin (*yes, I know all the wild family stories!*), my confidant, and my biggest cheerleader. Her life's mission is to inspire others to live out their full, God-given potential.

As you turn the pages, you will be amazed and inspired. And remember, what God has done in the lives of these women, He can do in yours.

As a Christian radio Host, I know the power of sharing our stories to encourage others and to point people to Jesus. My prayer is that God will use the stories within this book to give you hope and excitement for your future!

- Darla Ozanne,
Morning Host and General Manager, Prayz Network

Strength and dignity are her clothing,
and she laughs at the time to come.
Proverbs 31:25 (ESV)

She Laughs Without Fear of Loss

God Accomplishes His Purposes

Katelyn Silva

So many people long to see into the future: the general future and their personal future. I believe part of it is out of a sense of fear, even pride; a belief that we are actually in control of our lives and that if we knew the future, we would be able to have victory over our circumstances. People chase prophecy claims with abandon, fall prey to false prophets, and are quick to believe someone who claims they "hear directly from God".

Don't get me wrong, I absolutely believe in hearing from God. But I'm getting ahead of myself.

The truth is: all of it is an illusion of control.

When I was at the precious age of eight, I lost my mom. Early journal entries of mine from that time show a very different sense of the world before and after her death, where afterward reflected a darkness and a great sense of confusion and uncertainty.

As I grew older, my sense of self became very divided. My dad moved me and my younger siblings halfway across the country to a new home. I believe it was a fresh start for him. But it left us feeling alone without a sense of community and belonging in that new environment, without a history of people who deeply understood us and who we were.

In that place, I was responsible for helping care for my younger siblings. Part of my identity was being the responsible one, the dependable one, the one who figured out how to get things done, no matter what. Keep the home, maintain grades, help my siblings to the best of my ability. That was my expectation.

There were beautiful other moms who tried to step in, some I will never forget for their kindness and support and the impact they left in that time. But each of them eventually moved out of our lives, leaving us acutely aware of what we were missing, because a mother can never truly be replaced.

Another part of my identity was in seeking out "love" in boys. Can you relate? It was a path with loss of innocence, broken hearts, and violation. A path that opened doors of deep struggle in my life for over a decade and I daresay even demonic doors of deception.

Amidst all of this, there was a deep part of me that still clung to the dreams of my life before I lost my mom. The one that always said, "When I grow up, I'll be a mom and an author." She encouraged my creativity. She demonstrated such strong faith even leading up to her death. And this part of me was another identity I held when I wasn't seeking the love and approval of anyone else. It was who I was when I could just be.

When I was eighteen, I went through one of the darkest times in my life. I was recovering from rape, breakup, loss of a sense of family and friends, uncertainty, questioning my future, and deeply troubling things happening at home. My grades were slipping, I was in a deep depression, even my countenance was dark – looking back. I turned to some family I thought I could trust. The next few months were a daily assault of verbal abuse. When I finally left that environment, my self-esteem was absolute zero. Even a joke sent me into a self-hating torrent.

In that time, I asked a friend, "Why am I going through this?"

She said something that struck me deeply and that I've carried since. "God has plans to use your suffering for good. When you get through this, you will use it and help others."

Some people have criticized this type of advice for someone suffering… but for me, it was hope. It was meaning and purpose and a light at the end of the very dark tunnel I was in at the time.

It was also during that time that I met my husband, and thus began my journey into understanding the beauty in the sovereignty of God.

 Despite these pieces, God was still preparing and molding me into who He made me to be. And I still had much to surrender and turn and heal from.

My husband and I became consumed with growing our family and paying the bills and learning how to live life together. We had two little mouths to feed and limited income and big hopes and dreams for the future. Amidst all that, that core identity within me got buried and placed aside.

Yet there was a promise between us. I longed to be a stay-at-home mom to my babies and teach them for the time I had with them. "Just work for a few years until I can get stable, and then you can stay home," my husband told me. I clung to that.

At the time, my husband had a financial consulting business, and things were starting to look up. There was a big contract in the works, all was aligning. Overnight (quite literally), he went from being about to close his biggest contract, to receiving a phone call the next day that the company had sold to a new owner, and he would need to start the entire process again from zero.

The door was slammed in his face.

We pivoted. I said, "I will support you in whatever you do, as long as it's something you love." I didn't want him to slave away, watching his life drain from him. I wanted him to do something that excited him, something he excelled in and enjoyed.

He decided to go back to school for nursing. That meant a smaller local college nursing program with a reputation for low graduate rates because of the level of demand on the students and the rigidness of the grading for clinicals. During that same time, one of our dogs had puppies. It was exciting, fun, and hopeful for the future.

But we didn't live in the best neighborhood, including drug dealers right next door. Of all days, the one right before one of the biggest clinical trials of the semester – one that would determine my husband's ability to get his nursing license in the state because of the nature of the program – our mama dog suddenly went into seizures and passed away. The vet ran some tests and reported it was rat poisoning. We suspected our dealer neighbors had chucked it into our yard and that poor mama had eaten all of it to protect her babies.

My husband was devastated.

This wasn't our first dog loss, but it was the hardest one.

Needless to say, he failed the clinical and was removed from the program.

Now what?

He was able to get into a nursing program in another state and we moved two hours away. New town. New home. New job. New daycare. And no one we knew for the second time in my life.

Amidst all of it, God still showed up. On the absolute last possible day, God provided exactly the rent home (within our budget) and daycare for our babies that we needed. We were able to move everything and get started within a two-day time frame.

Looking back, I needed that reminder that God was with me and that I could depend on Him.

I still wasn't where He wanted me though.

I was undisciplined, faithless, and I had compromised my fire for him to placate my employers. Fear of man and losing my job (and thereby having uncertainty for my family) were leading me more than faith.

At the same time, I knew within my core who I was supposed to be and what I was supposed to be doing. The burning desire for writing and motherhood was growing stronger. Then one day my son, who was getting close to the same age I was when my mom passed, had one of those child events at school where they perform with a cute dance and some songs.

I was working, so I missed it.

When I arrived to pick him up after school, he looked up at me with tears in his eyes and he said, "Mama, where were you? I looked around and saw all my friends' parents but I couldn't find you."

My heart shattered in that moment and like a sucker punch to the gut, I thought, *'What am I doing? What if I look back in twenty years with regret, wishing I had done what I knew I was supposed to be doing all along? What if I miss out on all those once-in-a-lifetime moments with my babies I'll never get back? What if something happens to me and all my babies remember is me working?'*

I had a vision of working from home, impacting people, sharing my ideas, and being a mom all at the same time. I don't mean a divinely placed, "This is God showing me my future," type of vision. More like a deep desire within my heart that was lit on fire.

The problem was, my husband still had two years left of nursing school and emotionally speaking, I was burnt out from my job. I was ready for the change *now.*

Instead of seeking the Lord and patiently waiting and trusting His plan and timing, I went behind my husband's back and launched my own business, believing that in my own ability, I would replace my income, get to stay home, and all my dreams would come true!

I got way ahead of God, and even announced I would be leaving the company I had worked for in my brazen pursuit.

It could have ended very, very badly. Not only did the business *not* take off, but every effort I made slammed shut in my face. It was going down fast. My husband and I made an agreement. Either my business took off by the beginning of the next year, or I went back to work.

I wasn't sure what I was going to do, considering I had already burned the work bridge, and my position had already been replaced.

By that point, we were only one semester away from my husband finishing nursing school and being able to start work as a nurse full-time. I reached out to my former supervisor. He told me that they had full openings at a company location in the town we had originally moved away from (and were moving back to after my husband's schooling), and that the supervisor of the area who had been a huge part of my training wanted to take me on board.

Not only that, I found out that one of the fellow managers I had already worked with and trusted would be coming in with me as the general manager above me, and that she and I would be working together as a team. Furthermore, he informed me there had been an error in the system when I had parted ways, and that I could transfer seamlessly as if I had never left. I could go back to work just like that.

I moved back to the other town while my husband finished his nursing school semester, and once again, God provided living and a daycare for my youngest right on time when I needed it – my oldest was in school so he stayed with my husband to finish the semester.

Finally, we were together again. But because of my own foolishness, I couldn't just immediately stop working and go full-time at home. Worse, I still wasn't exactly following the path of righteousness. Remember those demonic doors of deception I mentioned? They still had full sway in my life where I was chasing after everything that wasn't of God.

After getting ahead of God and jumping into the world of online business without proper covering, I was led into all kinds of various "business" teachings for success. I became obsessed with learning how to become a millionaire, how to "manifest" my desires through positive affirmations, vision boards, and Eastern meditation. I started believing the teachings of those such as Wallace D. Wattles, Florence Scovel Shinn, and Eckhart Tolle. I was trying to align my chakras and open my third eye.

I even experienced receiving some of the things I tried to "manifest", making me believe even more. I started wrestling with God. *'God, what is this? Is it truly in your word? Is it truly of you? I'm so confused. There is power here. There is reality here. But what is it?'*

See, the problem was I was so out of touch with God's word, I didn't even recognize how those I was following were taking Scripture out of context and twisting it to share their teachings. I fell for the lie that because they were using a Bible verse, it must be right.

I truly believe that even then, God kept me and protected me. He was good to me when I was faithless.

Despite all of these things, I'll never forget the day my husband said, "You can stay home."

During the same year I returned to work while my husband was getting established working full-time as a nurse, we had three devastating miscarriages. But all of it led to my beautiful daughter, who I became pregnant with right after the third loss. She was our gift, our rainbow baby. Before I could even take a test to confirm, I knew I was pregnant and that it was a girl and that I wasn't going to lose her. I had dreams of holding a beautiful baby girl before I could even get an ultrasound.

When she was born, I looked into her eyes and I told my husband, "I can't put her in daycare." I couldn't. I didn't want to miss one second of being her mom.

In the last week of my postpartum recovery, as my husband and I were talking about whether or not I would return to work, the day finally came for me to shift into being a full-time mom. (And author.) The Lord answered these cries of my heart, and I began the transition from full-time manager to learning how to take care of my home and babies. It took time. In all of it, I was still pursuing the deceptive teachings and looking everywhere for spiritual growth *except* the Bible.

One step at a time, God was actually leading. He was preparing me and showing me the difference between the world's way and His way. At long last, there was one night after I put the kids to bed where I was watching videos on YouTube and I saw one that said, "New Age to Jesus."

'I don't need to watch that. I already have Jesus,' I thought.

But the Holy Spirit pressed my spirit. "You need to watch this."

'Nah, I'm good.'

"Watch this now."

I hesitated. I debated. And finally, I obeyed.

The girl on the video started sharing her testimony. With every single word, I was rocked to my core. Completely shaken. Her testimony was mine. Raised in a Christian home. Received Jesus at a young age. Taught the Bible. But led into deception until she watched a testimony, just like I was doing right then.

In that moment, the tangible presence of God stepped into the room. I was absolutely broken and weeping in repentance. In that one moment, figurative scales fell from my eyes. I could see so clearly all of the deception, all of my mistakes, everything I had been believing that was wrong, how the enemy has infiltrated so many facets of our culture and society, including the church, with these teachings, and how incredibly idolatrous and foolish I had been.

In that moment, God completely cleansed me and absolutely set my soul on fire for Him. He purged me, transformed me, and made me new. I started devouring my Bible like someone who's been starving and is suddenly presented with a feast.

I read and understood like never before in my life because of the Holy Spirit guiding me.

I literally didn't recognize the person I had been before. There was no desire for the sins that had tempted and enslaved me. I was disgusted by them! There was only desire for Jesus and His Word and holiness and pleasing Him!

Everything started to shift dramatically after that.

I asked God, "Why did you let me walk through that?"

He said, "So that you can now use your testimony to help and warn and teach others."

I asked God, "What do you want me to do with what you've given me?"

He said, "Write, darling girl, write."

The Lord started moving powerfully. He started connecting me with other believers who are on fire for Him; people I had seen in certain circles and thought there was no way they would ever receive and acknowledge me. They did! God led me through a season of purging and breaking off every lie, every wrong, every entrapment I had. I came to a moment of such complete surrender that He asked me to lay *everything* completely at His feet. "If all you ever accomplished was being a good mom, I want that to be good enough for you."

"Thy will be done, Lord! I lay it at your feet. All of it. My business. My dreams. My ambitions. My writing. Take it. What would you have me do?"

There was much uncertainty in that time. For two weeks, I was in limbo, not sure what next steps to take. I reached a point where I would either move forward or completely shut everything down.

At last, I asked God, "Lord, I need your answer. Do you want me to give it all up? Or not? If you want me to keep going in business, I need a client this week. And if not, I am going to stop completely."

That very week, I received a phone call from someone seemingly out of the blue. He said, "God told me to hire you." He is now an ongoing client I am so blessed God sent! My smile that day must have been from ear to ear. Tears of joy literally fell. From that moment, God started leading me step-by-step. He opened doors and closed doors one at a time. He provided exactly where He wanted me to go and when.

Where I had rigidly planned my life every day before, He led me into a season of relying on Him day by day and having no plan other than obedience to His leading. It was not easy.

God started bringing the right people into my life in sequence, whispering to my spirit, "This is who I wanted you to meet."

Things I had never grown up being taught or hearing about or seeing, but that are all over the Bible, were introduced to me. I was led by the Holy Spirit into a 21-day fast with liquids only. I was uncertain, as I was nursing at the time, but as I was on a run, He said so clearly, "I am the God who sustained Moses on the mountain for 40 days with neither food nor water. I gave the Israelites manna from heaven in the wilderness and water from a rock. I am Almighty God, Creator of the universe. I can sustain you and your baby."

And He did!

Through that, God used it to bring other women around me to Himself in radical new ways also. God led me to deeper intimacy with Him – intimacy I had never known about! I started learning about being baptized with the Holy Spirit and fire, and understanding what it means when Jesus said:

"And I tell you, ask, and it will be given to you; seek, and you will find; knock, and it will be opened to you. For everyone who asks receives, and the one who seeks finds, and to the one who knocks it will be opened. What father among you, if his son asks for a fish, will instead of a fish give him a serpent; or if he asks for an egg, will give him a scorpion? If you then, who are evil, know how to give good gifts to your children, how much more will the heavenly Father give the Holy Spirit to those who ask him!" Luke 11:9-13 ESV

And when Paul said to earnestly desire the greater gifts as in 1 Corinthians 12.

I started to daily seek the Lord and pray for these things. And He answered. I received the gift of praying in a new tongue, as in when Paul said, "Now I want all of you to speak in a tongue…I thank God I speak in a tongue more than all of you." 1 Corinthians 14:5, 8.

Paul has much more to say there, and I encourage you to read all of it. I made dramatic shifts in my approach. I grew in boldness. I started purging my business of anything displeasing to God. This opened the door to even more divine connections.

I was invited to what I thought was a business conference and God made the way to go. Even beforehand, He told me He had something for me there.

When I walked into that room, the tangible presence of God was a weight in the atmosphere. My response was to get on my knees and pray and give Him glory! It was at that event that I witnessed firsthand the true power and authority of Jesus and His name. I saw demons cast out. I saw real life instant healing.

But it wasn't just seeing it for others.

What I hadn't shared with anyone outside of my husband and children was the chronic back pain I had been living with for *years*. It had gotten to the point where I was desperate and felt I had no solutions. I didn't go to the event for healing or for deliverance or for anything except to just meet a friend and find out what God had for me there.

Instead I had a radical encounter with God, just like when I was weeping in repentance. This time, though, it was to set me on the new path He had for me, unchained from every lie of the past. The Holy Spirit prompted me during one of the speaker's prayers to search for my back pain, and to my utter shock – it was gone!

Was it possible? Dared I believe it? But it was! I was absolutely gushing. The next morning, I discovered the pain had moved to my lower neck, which was quite odd. I asked the lady to pray for me again, and she told me that if it was moving around, that it was a spirit and not physical. *What?!* She laid hands on me along with my friend and rebuked the spirit and instantly I felt it moving in my neck and then I felt it leave my mouth. It was a strange experience to say the least!

But after the event, I was moving about my home and I stretched and heard a loud pop in my back and ever since I have not only been completely pain-free, but my husband was a witness to the change because I was able to start exercising and lifting weights as his partner in ways and levels that had been completely impossible before. Praise the Lord!

At that event, I re-dedicated my life to the Lord and was re-baptized along with many others, but specifically two beloved sisters in Christ who are absolute treasures to me. I went from longing to share the gospel but having so much uncertainty as to how before the event, to boldly just opening my mouth and sharing what I have seen and heard and the gospel of Jesus Christ to anyone I can.

The Lord opened my eyes to see and understand how He works the body of Christ together with their various gifts for purpose and for glory. One of my friends received a prophetic word of knowledge that a couple also there would have a baby where they hadn't been able to before. Nine months later, they welcomed their beautiful baby boy. This friend has an incredible and beautiful prophetic gift, which I have witnessed as truly from the Lord in many other occasions.

And as I continue to grow with the Lord, I have come to understand that He does indeed share what is coming and what He is doing. He does still speak through His prophets. He does reveal and guide and lead every single day. He does pour out the miraculous! But these are things that are meant to strengthen our faith, draw us closer to Him, and ultimately point us to the truth and the love of His Son Jesus. They're meant to be used to show the love and the power of God to bring the lost to Him!

God wants you to delight yourself in Him and He wants to also delight in you as His beloved. His sovereignty and providence is in the beautiful way He is with you in every moment to draw you to Himself. It is how He forms a wonderful mosaic over the course of each of our lives and decisions, both good and bad, that ultimately work His good will and plans. And it is how He sees, holds, and guides the future so that you can trust Him every single day, every single step.

Truly, to laugh without fear of the future is to rest in the joy, hope, and peace that passes understanding which comes from surrendering completely to God, and it is to know to your core the love He has for you.

Contact Information:
Katelyn Silva
6x International Bestselling Author. Speaker. Author Mentor.
www.wewritebooks.com
youtube.com/@coffeedatewithjesus

...with an ATTITUDE *of* GRATITUDE!

Melissa Eiserer

Attitude: *a settled way of thinking or feeling about someone or something, typically one that is reflected in a person's behavior.*

Gratitude: *the quality of being thankful; readiness to show appreciation for and to return kindness.*

Hello, Sunshine!

Are you walking in the sunlight for every step of your journey where you feel everything is peachy?

Or

Are you finding mountains too high to climb? Wading through deep valleys of trials and temptations? Is life dragging you down? Are you past the point of weary? Are your burdens too much tc shoulder anymore?

Yes, my friend, there are those things that drag us down on the daily. But let's talk about becoming a Proverbs 31 Woman so that we can laugh at the future by taking a STAND for our great, powerful, wonderful, and loving God!

Earlier this year I lost my main Proverbs 31 Woman role model, my 90-year-old mother, to Alzheimer's. I have to say that Alzheimer's is one of the most horrible diseases; it brings on all kinds of debilitating forms of Dementia and I would never wish it on anyone.

However, as our family was going through my mom's and dad's belongings and memoirs, I found a very special handwritten note to me from my oldest nephew (he's a year and eight months younger than me). He was probably around the age of eight when he wrote it. It said something to the effect of: "I'm sorry that I sassed you and I won't sass you again." I'm guessing we must have gotten into a battle of stubbornness?

Anyway, I got the biggest kick out of reading the little note because I knew that during our childhood we were told frequently not to "sass back!" Sass? Yes, I grew up sassy with a splash of attitude! It's not my fault (insert eye roll), being the youngest (much younger) of five children. My nieces and nephews are more like my cousins; we would argue like brothers and sisters sometimes, but I was their "aunt" and they "needed" to do what I said because I was the boss (or so I thought). We used the same words used on us by all the adults: "Don't you sass me."

Almost all of my siblings and their spouses are old enough to be my parents, so imagine growing up with nearly five sets of parents, or aunts and uncles, telling you what to do all the time. Ugh! Yep, bring out the sass, and let's be bossy for a while!

On my birthday this past winter, one of my beautiful, go-getter, sister-in-laws gave me a gift bag with some wonderful and fun items in it. However, there was this one item that suited me to a tee. It was a coffee cup with a very fitting quote that read: "Some Days I am a Princess, Some Days I am a Warrior (Choose Wisely)." This brought a smile to my face and I laughed because it was true! I love to be a princess and happy all the time, pleasing to others, but look out for warrior mode when that sass might come out! However, the fun and joking mug reminded me that I am a Proverbs 31 Woman, a virtuous, God-fearing-Warrior. I may come off as a roughy-toughy sometimes, but I'm learning to rope that attitude with gratitude. I want to be a faithful, Godly, Warrior, just like my grandmothers, mother, sisters, and sisters-in-law. I've been blessed, so blessed, with these Proverbs 31 Women as role models in fifty-four years. I have sass, attitude, and a work-hard mindset, yes, but I've learned to channel that into God's will, not my will. I will cherish the cup, and the one that gave it to me, for it couldn't have come at a better time in my life where in a few short weeks I would say my "see ya later's" to my momma as she made her way home to her Lord and Savior. My momma is now gone but golly am I blessed to have had mom as my Proverbs 31 Woman role model.

If there's a thing or two I've learned to be true about life, it's this: life is filled with *uncontrollables*. Losing loved ones, finances, or health, are very much uncontrollable situations in life. For some women (men too), the word uncontrollable brings to mind a lot of negative verbs like anxiety, worry, stress, tension, fear, and/or strain. For me, it's some of those, but agitation is a button I allow to be pushed within myself when I'm put into circumstances I may not be in control of. What happens when I become agitated? Well, it brings out that word I've been accused of a lot in my life, being sassy and/or edgy! Now as an adult woman, I like to think of my sassiness more as an energetic attitude with a plan to get the job done, because I will work like a Proverbs 31 Woman to be as prepared as I can for whatever life throws my way. The Holy Bible tells us that we are to be watchful and ready:

"Be dressed ready for service and keep your lamps burning"; Luke 12: 35 (NIVSB).

Furthermore, the descriptive word from the Bible that sums up all that sass, independence, and overconfidence portrayed is "Virtuous."

Virtuous, in the Bible, can be interpreted as a brave warrior. Proverbs 31:10-31 (KJV) reads: "Who can find a virtuous wife?" In this passage, we are looking at a *Godly Warrior*, a warrior wife. We are not seeing someone who is bad, hateful, or a killer going on a physical war path, but rather at a Proverbs 31 Woman Warrior of God! Let's take a look...

Who is she? What is she worth? What does she do? How does she model?

She is a woman who:

- Is noble
- Is worth more than rubies
- Has full confidence
- Is known for her value
- Brings good not harm
- Shops frugally
- Works willingly with her hands
- Prepares good food for her family
- Works vigorously and constantly, in the day and night, in her home and stays strong
- Buys farms and makes them profitable
- Makes sure her heart is ready for God
- Gives to others in need
- Does not fear the cold but clothes herself and her family well
- Makes sure her family is respected
- Is worthy of praise
- Has strength and dignity so she can laugh at the days to come
- Speaks with wisdom
- Is a faithful instructor
- Models work, not idleness
- Her children and husband arise and call her blessed
- Her husband praises her and lets her know that he thinks she is *the best*

- Her biggest, most *valued* accolade she wants to be known for is that... she is a woman who fears the Lord!

A woman who fears the Lord; that is what she is known and praised for. She is working for the Lord. She is honored for her work on earth. She is a warrior who is ready to put on the Armor of God (Ephesians 6:10-19), and to serve Him as He leads her with the power of the salvation of His son Jesus and the power of His Holy Spirit to protect her family. This! This Proverbs 31 Woman is who I aspire to be! If we can be this Proverbs 31 Woman, then we can battle the *uncontrollables* in life that bring on all those negative words we often use to label ourselves with.

I laugh at the future, for there is *hope*. I *know* God is the *light* and in Him there is *no* darkness! 1 John 1:5: I can look to Him to be the light I need in this world. I take a stand and put my trust in the Lord, he is my true hope.

Going to Battle Against the Uncontrollables

Uncontrollables: things that cannot be managed or influenced.

To become a Proverbs 31 Woman means taking on some new vocabulary. These new words help you stand strong and to "be ready" when Uncontrollables come along in life.

Colossians 3:5b instructs: "Put to death, therefore, whatever belongs to your earthly nature." So ditch the negative vibes and focus on the positive virtuous words that have you living as one made alive in Christ.

"Therefore, as God's chosen people, holy and dearly loved, clothe yourselves with compassion, kindness, humility, gentleness, and patience. Bear with each other and forgive one another if any of you has a grievance against someone. Forgive as the Lord forgave you. And over all these "Virtues" put on *love*, which binds them all together in perfect unity. Let the peace of Christ rule in your hearts, since as members of one body you were called to peace. And *be thankful*. Let the *message of Christ* dwell among you richly as you teach and admonish one another with all wisdom through psalms, hymns, and songs from the Spirit; singing to God with gratitude in your hearts. And whatever you do, whether in word or deed, do it all in the name of the Lord Jesus, giving thanks to God the Father through him" Colossians 3:12-17.

Cultivate these new things and form habits to strengthen your walk with God.

Be *intentional*!

Go to Battle Being Intentional

Intentional: *done on purpose or deliberately.*

At the start of each new year, for about the last three years, instead of setting a New Year's Resolution I decided to set goals and choose a word for the year. Last year I chose the word INTENTIONAL. I liked it so much that I adopted it as a new part of my daily life routine.

A well-decorated and honored general doesn't go into battle unprepared. He or she takes time to set goals, plan, train, and carry out their mission with intention. The general prepares the troops to do the same.

As a woman warrior for God, what might your intentions look like? How can you become the Proverbs 31 Woman Warrior you want to be? How can you train to be this woman? Well – you plan.

The same sister-in-law who gave me the coffee mug gave me a black and white picture of a cowgirl in her rhinestone-fringed hat and dress with a lariat that read, "Actually, this is my first rodeo." She's so funny, and she loves a good laugh. (I just love her gifts as they make me laugh too.) Everyone needs a sister-in-law like mine; well unless she's in her *intentional* clean-up mode after a family dinner. Then hang on to your tea glass; she'll be hunting it down! Guess what, Sister? We are all in the same "first rodeo" known as the beautiful thing called life! So be *intentional*. Set goals. Plan. Be prepared for whatever life's rodeo throws your way; whatever battle you go through. Put God's word in front of you every day so that you are armored up for the day's rodeo.

The following is only a suggestion for you but is my daily personal plan that keeps me grounded as a Proverbs 31 Woman:

An Intentional Plan for a Proverbs 31 Woman:

1.	*Rise early.*
2.	*Start your day in a Prayer Life with God saying Prayers of Praise: make a list of praises and concerns to pray over. I use my church bulletin prayer list and add to it every week.*
3.	*Daily Devotions help build a relationship with Jesus. Use an app like YouVersion or seek out pastors who do live devotions on social media. Don't forget to hit that "share" button and post to your feed/story; this is your "field to sow seed" so that God's Word is shared by you with others. I post to Facebook, Instagram, X, Threads, etc...*
4.	*Study the Holy Bible: have a physical bible study that you can do by yourself or that you may be doing in a small group. Intentionally study every day to stay grounded in His word. First thing in the morning is a great way to start your day but get it in before bed. This is a great way to listen and discern what God's intentions are in your life and be led by the Holy Spirit.*
5.	*Pray over your meals (no matter where you are): it cultivates gratefulness.*
6.	*Do your daily chores, jobs, and look after your household with joy: praise and blessings are your reward.*

7.	*Take good physical care of yourself: stay strong so that you can care for others.*
8.	*Be respectful: speak with wisdom and faith.*
9.	*Fear the Lord: say your nightly prayers giving thanks to God.*
10.	*Do these things to keep your lamps trimmed and ready for the Lord's coming.*

Another aspect of staying prepared and planning ahead is to determine your daily attitude.

*As a Proverbs 31 Woman, which of the following examples of a woman of attitude will you strive to embrace and demonstrate to others during uncontrollable moments in life? (The following starred * quotes or sayings are the refrigerator magnets that make me laugh and/or are uplifting and give me strength.)*

<u>Example 1</u>: *the negative warrior - armed and ready to bring on a fight to bring her own justice.*

Will you be a negative attitude type of woman to think or say the following types of things?

*I'm only talking to my Dog today.
*I didn't mean to push all your buttons, I was just looking for mute.

Or

<u>Example 2:</u> *the positive Proverbs 31 Woman Warrior of God - powered by the Armor of God and ready to bring on life's rodeo and the Great Commissions God has discipled her to be ready for.*

Will you be a positive attitude type of woman to think or say the following types of things?

*She believed He could, so she prayed.

*Lord grant me the diligence to find answers to the questions that can be answered, faith to accept the ones that cannot (uncontrollables), and the wisdom to know the difference.

A Proverbs 31 woman might have uncontrollables in her life but she is equipped to handle those moments because she does the things that honor God; she has a firm relationship with Jesus Christ; and she listens to, discerns, and allows the Holy Spirit to guide her all of her days.

My prayer for you as a Proverbs 31 Woman Warrior is that you look for and find God's truth in every season of life's "rodeos." May you be intentional, set goals, plan, and be prepared for any battle. May you cultivate healthy habits by taking negative emotions out of the situation and putting *Jesus* in it. May you always be thankful, grateful, and blessed. May you wear strength and honor as your clothing. May you laugh at the future living the life of a Proverbs 31 Woman who fears that Lord. May your journey always lead you "home". We are all in this together and I want to encourage you to find your tribe, your circle, your sisters (and brothers) in Christ and meet with them *regularly* to stay lifted up in Christ-filled relationships. May the God of *hope* fill you with all *joy* and *peace* as you trust in *Him* (Romans 15:13). In Christ's Holy Name, Amen.

Well, Sunshine, I hope you laugh at the future with an *Attitude* of *Gratitude*! And while you're riding out the rodeo of life don't forget to sing a little along the way. Here's one of my favorite choruses I'm sure you'll know, so sing along...

> So RISE and SHINE and give GOD the GLORY, GLORY.
> RISE and SHINE and give GOD the GLORY, GLORY.
> RISE AND SHINE AND give GOD the GLORY, GLORY. Children of the Lord!

Contact Information:
Melissa Eiserer
Christian Career Coach, Consultant and Speaker
Email: meiserercoaching3@gmail.com
Facebook: Melissa Eiserer, Career Coaching & Consulting

From Frustration to Peace:
A Story of Forgiveness

Helen Corban

I never thought I could get to true peace, but somehow, I have. Only by the love and grace of God, and the outstanding people in my life - who have stood by me, supported me, and shown me the way - have I managed to learn to hand over my pain, frustration, and sometimes pure heartbreak to God.

I'd like to tell you that forgiveness has been easy for me. That I can miraculously forgive because I have God's forgiveness. However, forgiving the big stuff, the hard stuff, the things I did not deserve, and forgiving myself has been a long process for me.

I've wrestled with questions such as:

-       When you have been wronged and can never solve that injustice, how do you let go of it?
-       How do you forgive when you are so angry because the other person will never change, and they have hurt you?
-       How do you get to a place where you feel peace towards those people who have lied about situations?

-        How do you really know when you have forgiven?
-        When do you know in your heart you have truly let those things that hurt you go?

What is forgiveness?

It is the process of consciously deciding to let go of resentment, anger, or the desire for revenge toward someone who has wronged you, even if they don't deserve it. Forgiveness does not necessarily mean reconciling with the person who caused the harm or condoning their actions, but it is about freeing oneself from the burden of past grievances.

In a Christian context, forgiveness is both a command and a reflection of God's grace. As Christians, forgiveness is central to the belief that God has forgiven us through the sacrifice of Jesus on the cross. Therefore, we are called to forgive others as God has forgiven us, regardless of the severity of the incident.

Christian forgiveness is not just about letting go of resentment but also involves an active choice to love and pray for those who have wronged us, aiming for reconciliation whenever possible. Forgiveness is a gift from God. So that we can live freely. Over the years I have prayed for people I have needed to forgive, even through my tears.

Why is forgiveness so important? If we have unforgiveness it keeps us a prisoner of the past. Forgiveness releases us.

"For if you forgive other people when they sin against you, your heavenly Father will also forgive you" (Matthew 6:14-15).

A popular saying goes: "Not forgiving is like drinking poison and expecting the other person to die." Without forgiveness, you live as a victim. Forgiveness is a conscious act, using your will. Without it, it is like a disease that erodes away at your heart. You need to decide to surrender any bitterness and vengeful thoughts and really let go. Unforgiveness stands between you and God. Not you and the person.

I have heard it said, "Apologize fast, forgive faster". When you forgive, you prioritize the relationship - saying it is more important than what happened. Isn't it amazing when someone forgives you without conditions? God has done that for me. I always want to be that person. I don't always have to win, but I know that if I want to be free, I always have to forgive.

Forgiveness is a strong, life-changing force and I have experienced that. It's a part of life that we slip up and make mistakes. Say the wrong thing, do the wrong thing, make bad decisions with difficult consequences. What is important is our response: correct ourselves, own it, and take full responsibility.

Love is the basis of forgiveness. Love forgives. There is no record keeping.

Psalm 130:3-4, "If you, Lord, kept a record of sins, Lord, who could stand? But with you there is forgiveness, so that we can, with reverence, serve you."

Love forgives by recognizing the value and worthiness in others, seeing past their faults and failures to the core of who they are. It doesn't dismiss or excuse wrongs, but it chooses to release resentment and the desire for revenge. Ultimately, the heart wants to restore relationships and promote healing.

Forgiveness through love is an act of grace, acknowledging that everyone is imperfect and that holding onto bitterness only prolongs pain. Love-driven forgiveness prioritizes the well-being of both the forgiver and the forgiven, aiming to bring peace and reconciliation. It's about choosing to let go of the past and allowing space for growth, both within yourself and in relationships.

In a faith-based context, love forgives because it understands that forgiveness is a reflection of God's love for us and divine grace. It's about unconditional love, something that is hard to see in our human lives. God's love offers a way to redemption and renewal.

1 Corinthians 13:7, "Love bears all things, believes all things, hopes all things, endures all things."

As Christians, we have new "mercies" every morning, and we can leave any unforgiveness behind. I love this. We can have a fresh start every day. Yesterday is gone. We can choose to do our best today.

Lamentations 3:22-23, "The steadfast love of the Lord never ceases; his mercies never come to an end; they are new every morning; great is your faithfulness."

I asked my sister and a few close friends how they have seen my journey of forgiveness.

Karen, my younger sister, said, "I have seen you choose to communicate with others despite the difficulties and pain... be honest and speak the truth in love. You choose the higher way. Sharing the love of Christ."

My oldest friend (over forty-six years of friendship) said, "I have always admired the way you are able to forgive and put things into perspective and treat whatever the situation was as a learning curve. You always wrote down your views in a letter format, then chose to either send or not send. Whilst I was usually raging for you, you calmly got it all out and moved on. All your experiences have made you a strong person."

Another friend of over thirty-five years said, "Your natural ability to empathize in a non-judgmental way has led to our long and honest friendship. Your never-ending love of supporting the community through volunteer work over the years, despite any personal hurdles, shows your true loving and forgiving heart. You can easily forgive."

Very kind words, though does that mean I have effortlessly forgiven others or myself? Not really. I have had to be very conscious about how I choose to interpret the situation through my anger or my tears many times.

There have been various people in my life who have shaped my journey of forgiveness and considerably influenced my life. Looking back now from a place of forgiveness and peace, I can see the learnings and appreciate the journey. Do I have sadness and regrets? Of course I do, but I choose my perspective, my attitude, and my outlook. Sadness and grief creep up on me at times. I use all the tools I have collected over the years to deal with those emotions, tools like prayer, reflection, writing things down, and talking things through with wise, trusted friends.

I have seen the results of a lack of forgiveness in people's lives, and it is not pretty. Actions that continually cause destructive dramas and dysfunction. They continue to make bad decisions as their filters are programmed to look for the worst, be cynical, and be suspicious. It is easy to see the anger, bitterness, and vitriol on their faces.

I met someone recently whose second husband had cheated on her, the same as her first husband. She was consumed with hatred, and this was after many years. The vengeful attitude and the expression on her face was just so sad to me. I did ask her about forgiving her ex-husband, and she said she would never, ever forgive. I have uttered those same words also in my life but took them back. I am grateful I did.

A Few Thoughts About My Mother

My mother was an obstetrician and gynecologist, and an incredibly accomplished woman. Powerful, driven, with a very strong work ethic.

Mum was a staunch atheist who used to proudly tell the story of how she visited quite a few churches of different religions at the age of seven and decided then that God was not real. I couldn't believe that Mum would stick with the opinions she made as a seven-year-old.

Mum was very strong in her opinions, and I was brought up to not respect religion in any form. Mum had a very strong mother as well, a trailblazer in many respects. My grandmother was one of the first women in New Zealand to achieve her Bachelor's degree in Education in 1921. Later in life, she travelled behind both the Iron Curtain to Moscow in the 1950s, and the Bamboo Curtain to China twice in the 1970s, although our family is not socialist. She was involved in environmental issues, abortion rights, gay rights, and Maori rights. My grandmother was neither gay nor Maori. A Maori group even did a *haka* at her funeral to honor her and show their respect. Looking back, it was all amazing. My mother came from that background and was extremely proud of her mother's staunch values, ideals, and achievements. Mum based a lot of her behavior on her mother.

My younger sister Karen suddenly became a Christian in 1985 when she was twenty-one years old; it seemed to come out of nowhere. She had been on a tough journey, somewhat self-destructive. My mother said it was as if there was a death in the family. I didn't understand my sister's new faith or my mother's extreme reaction to it.

In April 1995, at the age of thirty-two, just after returning to New Zealand from a two-year stint in Japan, I went on a trip around the country, and in Nelson, I became a Christian. There had been a visiting evangelical preacher at church, Tom Frew, an Irishman. He was telling the most hilarious irreverent jokes; I was laughing my head off. I then started crying a lot, and I wasn't sure why. My sister took me up to the front of the church and Tom held my hands and asked if I wanted to become a Christian. I said, "I don't know," through my tears, thinking being a Christian was very uncool. A few days later, at my sister's house, I gave my heart to Jesus.

Back in Auckland a few weeks later, I organized a party to commemorate twenty years since my father passed away from cancer in 1975. I love the way the Japanese remember and respect loved ones who have passed away so I thought this would be a great idea. It was an amazing party, and we managed to track down ex-colleagues and ex-students of Dad's. Dad was also a doctor, a general surgeon. I will never forget Mum coming into my room the day of the party and saying she had heard I had become a Christian. She proceeded to threaten me by saying she would cut me off (a common threat I didn't care about) and any children I had as well.

Mum did say things at times that turned my stomach over and made me feel sick. She was one of the scariest people I have known. Nothing was off-limits. Mum thought she could say anything to anyone, it didn't matter what it was. A complete lack of boundaries.

One thing I know now is that if I wasn't a Christian, I would have cut my mother out of my life years ago. There was such a long list of grievances - for my sister as well - of cruel, thoughtless words, actions, and incidents. "Conditional love" was at the top of the list. "If you do this, then this happens..."

Grievances included not being listened to, no apologies for unkind words or actions and not being able to discuss issues. For me, it is hard when things can't be talked through. Some things were completely unacceptable and looking back there was such incredible disbelief at the way she treated me and my sister.

In saying all this, I loved my mother despite the hard parts. I appreciate the lessons I learned. She was an amazing doctor and had a very successful career. She would go above and beyond with her patients, and whilst her bedside manner was not necessarily soft and empathetic, patients knew they would be looked after very well. Mum created many great things, with some chaos mixed in along the way! Mum was also hilarious in many respects and infamous.

For me, it was so interesting the day she died in December 2019. I got a call from her husband at 12pm on the last working day of the year before Christmas, saying Mum was having a heart episode and asking if I could pick up a friend of hers, who arrived from out of town to visit. So, I did that, and we went to the retirement village where Mum had just moved to eight days prior. By the time we arrived, we had missed her by ten minutes. She had passed away suddenly, peacefully and painlessly with her husband holding her hand. I had forgiven Mum many times over the years but in that moment, looking at my mother in her bed, no longer alive, any angst I felt towards my mother completely left me. I just said, "Oh Mum," through my tears. I totally forgave everything. Compassion was the only emotion left.

Forgiving doesn't mean you forget, though you can choose how you look at the bigger picture. Mum had very little emotional intelligence and did not know how to communicate well. She simply gave her opinion, and that was that. No discussion. And if you challenged her opinion, it was hardly ever worth it. My sister often graciously said that Mum did the best with what she had. I used to think that was just a cop-out for accepting her bad behavior. I now see that differently, with more understanding and grace towards Mum.

Forgiving also doesn't mean you need to keep putting yourself in unsafe situations. After some counseling, I put some strategies in place if things ever turned pear-shaped when spending time with my mother.

My Marriage

After a lot of traveling, I settled back in New Zealand and married in 2000. I knew there were going to be challenges with our strong personalities but I thought when we got married, we would become a team. Unfortunately, we never became a team and I ended the marriage finally in 2014. We had counseling on and off for over twelve years. I did not walk away lightly.
I am grateful that I continue to be friends with my ex-husband. We are still negotiating life together, supporting our children. We can laugh over a glass of wine and a platter together. Now and again we push each other's buttons, and I must forgive again. However, overall, I know him so well and can deal with any challenges we have quickly.

I am a person who likes structure in my life. I need to be organized as that keeps me safe. Yes, I've done the counseling to know this. I take responsibility for my decisions and behavior. I certainly haven't always got it right. I work hard to have no regrets and not dwell on the past.

From my marriage, after three miscarriages (another forgiveness journey), I have two children, James and Emma. They have been the absolute lights of my life, and I have been blessed so much by the privilege of becoming a mother at the ages of thirty-nine and forty-one years. I loved creating a life for my children and we spent seventeen years in the suburb of Pt Chevalier, Auckland. This was a wonderful time despite the challenges in my marriage. I was part of an amazing community that really did support one another well along the journey of parenthood.

As I reflect on the various details of my past I remember the good times and the hard times. The tears, the disappointment, the frustration, and the anger. I remember crying out at God. Wanting answers.

Now and again, I have been so angry at God about how some things have turned out. I have learned to "dig deep" and would rather be at peace with

God and those in my world than go the other way. The consequences of not forgiving are so much worse. I can see that so clearly. There are things I don't understand, especially with tragic untimely deaths. I have decided I will never truly understand God and the world, so I focus on what I can do, and do my best to support and help others around me.

One great thing for me at my church (LIFE Central - Auckland) was that I never felt judged for being a Christian woman leaving her husband. I had some great friends and a wonderful counselor there who supported me. I was often at church on my own with the kids, and this was always a time of rest for me. I could breathe and rest in God for a few hours amidst a busy and challenging life. I felt safe in His peaceful presence.

I'd like to be able to say that when challenging situations happened, I forgave instantly, though that would not be true. It took years to truly forgive a few situations 100%, and in 2022 I worked with a relationship coach in the United States (Kiki Clarke of Vibrant Life Coaching) on forgiving my ex-husband, specifically, and on forgiving myself. It was an eight-week engagement and was incredibly helpful. I think forgiving yourself is the hardest part, as we are often our worst critic and enemy.

The forgiveness steps that have worked for me are:

- Praying - putting things into a box, taping up the box, and putting that box, figuratively speaking, at the foot of the cross
- Writing an email/letter of all I want to truly say about a situation, not send it, and later deleting it
- Writing a list of things I needed to forgive others for
- Writing a list of things I needed to forgive myself for
- Reading and speaking out those lists over and over

These kinds of strategies have been so helpful to me over the years.
How has my faith supported me through these challenges?

I have become very good at handing my challenges over to God. In Christian speak, laying my burdens down. There are key scriptures which have grounded me in God's truth for my life. God has always placed fantastic people around me, both Christian and non-Christian. I am straight-up and direct. I am very "real" and have sometimes done things not really in line with what God would want for me over the years. I was described at my sixtieth in 2023 by a dear friend and an ex-pastor as one of "God's naughtiest daughters". I do have that mischievous humor and am often laughing at the silly things in life. As an extrovert, I have had my journey with partying too hard and making bad decisions. I am known to be gregarious, singing and occasionally dancing on tables. I am finally calming down a bit! I'd hate to fall off the table!

However, whatever I am doing, I always talk to God and feel His love and forgiveness even if I have pushed things too far. I want to honor God. My motto is to "always keep my side of the street clean" and live with integrity. I keep accounts short, with God and with people. I work to get over things quickly, to stop reliving any hurt, and move forward.

Life hasn't turned out how I thought it would and I will be forever growing and learning. That is part of my commitment to God, my family, my friends, and those I serve through my business.

I believe I am in a place now where my experiences and my responses to them have brought me to being clothed in strength and dignity. I have the fortitude and support to handle any situation. I truly know my future is bright and full of laughter.

Contact Information:
Helen Corban
Business, Time Management, and Leadership Expert & Coach.
www.reachpotential.co.nz.

Where True Freedom Lies

Patty Schaad

2021 was the best and worst year of my life. As the world wrestled with the fear and effects of a global pandemic, I was a 29-year-old woman living in the heart of New Jersey, where I spent the year questioning my sanity, my selfishness, my relationships, and God.

Growing up Roman Catholic, as a little girl and even then as a young woman, I believed that God's love was a reward for being a "good girl". This belief deeply shaped how I saw myself and my life. I thought I had to earn God's love and acceptance through my actions, tying my self-worth to my achievements. I constantly strived for perfection and sought approval, always wanting to be seen as a good daughter, a good employee, and a good person. Hearing, "You're doing a good job," was the highest praise for me. And for someone who built their entire belief system on the approval and need to be "good", the vaccine mandate or narrative in the workplace was a pretty formative experience and a catalyst for psychological paths that weren't beneficial to my well-being at all.

On September 9, 2021, President Biden exercised his independent unconstitutional authority to act as CEO of the Executive Branch of the United States Government. He mandated an Executive Order that Federal Employees must be fully vaccinated against COVID-19 by November 22, 2021, or be removed from federal service. As a government employee, the ultimatum was: comply with the vaccine mandate or lose my job. No one knows how much I cried that day; God does.

The reason I felt so devastated was that, up until that point, my work was my whole world. I had invested everything into my job, pouring my heart and soul into every task. My job as a financial management analyst at the Naval Air Warfare Center Aircraft Division wasn't just a job; it was a huge part of who I was. My job was everything to me. I tied my sense of self-worth and identity to my work, constantly striving for perfection and seeking validation as a good employee. So when the mandate came along it felt like it was a direct attack on everything I had worked for and who I had become.

Federal employees were told that there would be no test-out option, but workers would be able to receive a reasonable accommodation for limited medical and religious reasons. The same rules applied to all contractors that do business with the federal government.

While millions of people did not work at all or worked fewer hours because their employer closed or lost business during the coronavirus pandemic, I was in my sixth year of federal service as a financial management analyst for the Naval Air Warfare Center Aircraft Division, which provides a variety of services to the Department of Defense, other Federal agencies, and non-Federal customers as the steward of the ranges, test facilities, laboratories, and aircraft necessary to support the Navy's acquisition requirements.

I strived to provide exceptional financial support to the Support Equipment and Aircraft Launch and Recovery Departments. I readily accepted all tasks and consistently provided accurate, complete work products in a timely manner. I actively participated in resolving team conflicts during workload transition periods. I worked numerous hours of overtime long after traditional work hours were over and on the weekends. Most importantly, I performed my duties with respect, professionalism, integrity, compassion, and dedication. My ability to communicate with co-workers and all levels of management proved my commitment to the warfighter, my teammates, and the Department of Navy.

The next several weeks turned into months, the light in my eyes that used to burn so bright, started to burn out. I was advised that refusing to get the COVID-19 vaccination would result in disciplinary action up to and including termination. Agencies were told they must work expeditiously to fully vaccinate employees as quickly as possible and by no later than November 22, 2021.With the government-wide adoption and implementation of these vaccination requirements, agencies were no longer required to establish a screen-testing program for employees or on-site contractor employees who were not fully vaccinated.

I believe it's important to acknowledge that many of us found ourselves in a similar boat. A trend emerged across various private industries in the fall of 2021, who also chose to implement a vaccination mandate for their employees. These mandates reflected the growing emphasis on vaccination as a crucial tool in the fight against the COVID-19 pandemic. Yet, I couldn't shake the feeling of being swept into a collective decision that overlooked individual circumstances.

Our immediate supervisors implemented these policies without formally evaluating how our vaccination status might impact our specific work environments. While we had been asked about our vaccination status, there weren't discussions about other medical conditions that might affect a comprehensive risk assessment. Things like pre-existing conditions or other contagious diseases were left out of the equation.

It was hard to understand how these policies, as applied to our situations, actually benefited our colleagues' well-being, health, and safety. There were many questions unanswered. I was not the only one left wondering what criteria was being used for risk assessment. Without individualized assessments, we couldn't have meaningful conversations about how these policies applied to us or what assumptions were guiding them.

I remember emailing my direct supervisor in the middle of October 2021 about the COVID-19 vaccine and my desire was to be fully informed of all facts before going ahead and making a decision. I needed to ensure that there was no threat to my health, and I felt like all the information available to me through the workplace SharePoint or the CDC website at that time was not enough. I had questions about vaccine safety, liability in case of adverse reactions, and the risk of COVID-19 fatality should the unfortunate happen and I contract the virus versus the vaccine.

My supervisor responded and directed me to the CDC website, as the source for official government guidance, and emphasized to me that failure to comply would lead to disciplinary steps. The words that flowed from my supervisor seemed to carry the weight of a system that prioritized productivity over genuine concern for health and safety. My supervisor went on to inform me that I would need to attend an employee counseling and education session, that continued non-compliance would result in a short, 14-day suspension without pay, and that further non-compliance after the suspension would result in removal from federal service.

It was in that moment where consent felt coerced, where decisions felt forced rather than chosen. Where was the respect for consent? For the freedom to make informed choices without coercion? Didn't the leadership at my job know what consent means? It means to freely choose, without manipulation, without psychological coercion, without guilt tripping. Consent is not a matter of, "Did you say, yes?" but rather, "Given the circumstances, could you have said no?"

I believe there's only one thing we should be mandating and that's freedom. Opposing vaccine mandates is not equivalent to opposing vaccines. We should not have to choose between keeping a job or getting an experimental vaccine, something that we may not need, may not want, and may not believe in. I believe that the freedoms we let go of today are the freedoms our children will know nothing of. Whether you are vaccinated or unvaccinated, you can still stand for freedom of choice. One day, something will be mandated that you don't agree with – who will be there to take a stand with you?

So when the mandate for COVID-19 vaccination for federal employees was announced, I can still recall the tears that streamed down my face. I grappled with the weight of the mandate, the weight of its implications bearing down on me like a heavy burden. It was more than just a career choice; there was a battle going on in my heart. The vaccine mandate made me confront my character. I remember feeling tremendous fear. It was like I was unraveling the threads of who I really was. I felt like I was only at this job because I could work hard and I was nice to people. I felt like they didn't really care about me because if they did, how could this be happening? How could this be normal? I felt like I was losing my mind.

I was afraid of the vaccine at the same time that I was grappling with the mandate. My family was fighting over the vaccine: its safety and efficiency and also over the mandate. I had questions and no one had answers. I just wanted to make an informed choice and be respected and listened to. It didn't make sense that hugs and kisses suddenly became weapons and not visiting grandparents and family and friends became an act of love. Masks and social distance aren't love. I will never be convinced of that. The biggest blow to my heart was when my father disapproved of my choice to remain unvaccinated. I lost relationships with my grandparents, cousins, and friends due to my choice to be unvaccinated.

I never contracted the COVID-19 virus, yet it did affect me. It isolated me, keeping me from everyone I love. It took loved ones away, leaving a huge hole in my heart. It shattered my love life, my relationships with family and friends. It ruined my professional reputation and interpersonal relationships.

It was becoming harder and harder to concentrate and focus on work. I was experiencing excessive fear and worry all hours of the day. The fear was overwhelming, physically, emotionally, and mentally numbing. Sleep was replaced by the torment of waking up in the dead of night. My chest was tight with panic. I couldn't find the off button to stop thinking obsessively about being presented with the idea of having to take the COVID-19 vaccination against my will. All I kept thinking was that vaccinated doesn't mean immune and unvaccinated doesn't mean infected. If fully vaccinated can get it and spread it, why aren't they losing their jobs too? Mandates are unethical.

Leadership explained that the disciplinary procedures for non-compliance would take place after the New Year. By the middle of December 2021, the hopelessness was so heavy, the presence of suicide was on my mind. The weight of uncertainty, the burdens I carried, it felt too much to bear, as if I couldn't be alive anymore. I sent in my resignation letter on December 16th, 2021, with no hope for a future.

The year of 2021 was extremely tough and challenging, both personally and professionally, but I found myself in complete darkness in December 2021.

Yet, someone I barely knew at work and had no previous connection with, heard of my resignation letter, and gave me a call afterward. In a divine moment, this coworker told me how much God loves me and she offered a sincere prayer for peace and invited me to go to church with her. She gave me scripture to read and mediate on: Matthew 11:28-30, Jeremiah

29:11, Proverbs 3:5-6, Philippians 4:6-7, Romans 12:2, and 2 Timothy 1:7. Three days later, I met my coworker at her church, and I accepted Jesus as my Lord and Savior on December 19th, 2021.

In a critical time, where the pandemic had taken its toll on millions, whether they contracted the virus or not, I needed Jesus.

Jesus said that when we are weary, heavy-laden, or overburdened, to come to Him and He will give us rest. (Matthew 11:28) This scripture saved my life. Jesus said to come by faith, so I did. I knew that Jesus could save me if I just let Him. As simply as I can tell, I believed in the invitation of Jesus and my life has taken a miraculous turn.

The rest that Jesus offers us is mentally, emotionally, physically, and spiritually refreshing. Jesus invited me to learn how to do what I needed to do, in Him.

When I went back to work that Monday, December 20th, 2021, I withdrew my resignation letter and submitted paperwork to file for an exemption against the vaccine mandate for mental health. In Him, I had courage to be an advocate. In Him, I waged a courageous war for truth, sanity, and freedom. In Him, I brought light to the darkness. The stand that I had taken was no easy road. It wasn't a path paved by the approval of other employees or the promise of worldly success. This was a path, a call of virtuous Christ-like character and faith, where the most important battles have been fought for the sake of truth.

Since then, God has been showing me that being a Christian isn't about doing good works. I do not have to earn God's love. His love is a gift, freely given through the sacrifice of Jesus Christ. Because of Jesus' sacrifice, I've received unconditional love, which has freed me from the constant pressure to be "good enough". I am now living in accordance with His invitation in Matthew 11:28, finding true fulfillment, purpose, and joy. I have shed the identity of a "good girl" and I am embracing my journey as a disciple of Jesus Christ. A disciple of joy and service to others. Who I was before I turned to Jesus and who I am today are two very different people. I wouldn't have the testimony I do in Jesus today if it wasn't for that period of darkness I went through. Jesus is the light that brought me out of the darkness. I am beyond grateful for the light that Jesus brings to my life.

I was donated three months' worth of leave from twenty-seven coworkers so that I could take a sabbatical beginning in late January 2022. These twenty-seven people listened to me without judgement, spoke to me without prejudice, helped me without entitlement, understood me without pretension, and loved me without any conditions. They sent me flowers and baskets of baked goodies and fruit. It was the first time since lockdown that I felt loved.

It was during my sabbatical, that God allowed me to remember how excited I used to be about the future, about life yet to be discovered, about opportunities yet to be claimed. I believe COVID-19 made my once clear vision fade into darkness; it made the future uncertain, seemingly unreachable, and hopeless. I missed the little girl whose dreams had no barriers, who believed in a world where anything is possible, and who had a heart full and unbroken. Jesus restored this little girl's dreams and made her heart full of hope again.

I started my pet sitting business on January 23, 2022 due to my love for dogs, and its success became a saving grace for me during that dark period. God gave me the courage to become a fearless entrepreneur and placed a call on my life of serving others. He encouraged me to dream big impossible dreams. Set big spiritual goals. Pray big prayers and expect bigger answers. (Ephesians 3:20-21) Failure doesn't exist in this business. I know this is where God wants to use me and make a difference.

At the end of my sabbatical, I went back to receive a new position under new leadership. Although the leadership still leaves a lot to be desired, I laugh at the future because I have learned that there is a blessing on the other side of brokenness. The breaking that was done in me allowed me to let go of all the accolades and titles, shed the good girl identity and just be happy with His presence. I only want what He wants for me. There is no job, no relationship, no school, and no object, that is worth losing who you are because somewhere, God ordained an opportunity waiting for the real you. I also laugh at the future because my resume can tell you where I've been, but you cannot define my life based on that. The best part of my story is with Jesus.

On August 3, 2022, the CDC announced that it would no longer differentiate between COVID-vaccinated and unvaccinated individuals. Every employee fired for being unvaccinated should be given their job back with a formal apology.

On March 2, 2024, the CDC revised their COVID guidelines, to treat COVID like the flu. Some of y'all still owe your family and friends an apology. It is time to mend those relationships. No more dividing lines. Your vaccination status doesn't change how much God loves you, or how much I do.

I laugh at the future because I no longer have to endure what once held me down, shook me around, and stole my peace. The coronavirus pandemic unleashed chaos on a global scale, its effects stretching far beyond the reach of the virus itself. Through it all, I've realized how deeply I have always wanted to live a life of freedom. God wants me to be happy every day and be joyful every day and be of sound mind every day. I'm more determined than ever to live this truth. I laugh at the future with courage and hope. I laugh because I know that God's presence is with me always. My heart is open and willing to go where He leads me-no matter the cost. And the most beautiful thing is that every place I go in this life,

He is there with me. As a fearless entrepreneur, I trust there is a God above who loves me more than I will ever know and who has called me to the work I do for a purpose greater than myself.

I am a Christian pet sitter whose mission is to bring God's love and care to furry friends near and far. I have a heart full of faith and passion for animals and I offer trusted and reliable pet sitting services that ensure pets are happy, safe, and loved while pet parents are away. I keep Jesus Christ at the center of my business, and I am in business to make someone's life better; to lift burdens. My core company values are faith, passion, helpfulness, and contribution.

This journey of becoming a fearless entrepreneur is light and full of love. Two years into this pet sitting adventure and my heart overflows with gratitude for Gods goodness. I am experiencing a complete restoration in my life! There is true fulfillment, purpose, and joy that is beyond words. And God is showing me that there are even greater and stronger blessings and opportunities yet to come in my fearless entrepreneur adventure!

I pray my story encourages you to face challenges with courage and faith. I pray that you never lose the vision of what the years to come could be. I pray that no matter how dark the days may look, that you have the courage within to dream. I pray that you hold onto this truth: courage comes from the presence of God. There is no place you've ever been that He was not there, and there is no place you will ever go where He will not be beside you. I pray that the revelation of this promise will allow your faith to grow and deliver you from fear as you step out into the calling God has placed on your life. True freedom comes from trusting in God's plan and embracing the journey He has for you. Remember the truth in Proverbs 31:25, "She is clothed with strength and dignity; she can laugh at the days to come." In Him, you are one woman who is stronger than you have ever thought possible, and in Him, you will always find freedom.

Contact Information:
Patricia "Patty" Grace Schaad
Patty's Pawsitivity
www.facebook.com/pattyspawsitivity

A Future Filled With Hope

Audrey Ostoyic

I had played out how the suicide note would read for days in my mind, and how the apology notes still needed to be written. I knew my children would go live with their dads. I just had to finish cleaning the home so that when everyone flew in or arrived for the service, the house would be clean, and it would be easy for my husband Billy to sell it and move on.

As I was on my hands and knees scrubbing the floor all I could do was cry out in anguish and scream at a God I didn't want to believe in anymore.

How did I get to this place of such hopelessness that suicide was the only answer?

More importantly, how did God raise me up out of those ashes of hopelessness to a faith that won't be shaken?

To answer these questions, let's go back to the future 2005 style.

It was November 2005 when Mom was making the rounds of calling each of us six kids to give us the news that her doctor just gave her.

Cancer! Stage 4! Chemo & Radiation. Not sure how long she has.

That is all I heard! Even though Mom was still talking, all I could focus on was the diagnosis.

'This can't be happening!' My mom was my best friend, my confidant, my prayer partner, my mentor, my voice of reason, my everything!

'God, please no!'

After the initial shock of it all wore off, I quickly went into the only stance I knew: the stance of a prayer warrior. I began decreeing and declaring God's word over her and coming into agreement with her that...

"She shall live and not die and will declare the works of the Lord." That "by Jesus's stripes she was healed, and we would just be waiting on the manifestation of her healing."

I knew God was no respecter of persons and what He did for Joel Osteen's mom He would do for my mom. She was diagnosed with the same form of cancer as Jodi Osteen so I just knew she was going to be healed also.

After adding her to every prayer request form we knew of, we stood together on God's word for her complete healing on this earth.

I'll never forget one Wednesday evening while driving to church after one of her doctor appointments, my mom called to ask me for a huge favor.

Of course I said, "Yes," without hesitation.

She asked me to not waver in faith and stand on God's word with her for complete healing in her body *despite* what the doctors and everyone else were saying.

She proceeded to tell me that there were lesions on her liver that the doctors wanted to remove but they would have to do it in two separate surgeries. First the right liver, then the left liver. The surgery would take place in Tampa at the Moffitt Center, and she would need to stay with me since I lived closest to the hospital at the time.

So, the summer of 2006, Mom came to stay with me for a little over a month until she felt strong enough to head back home and be with Dad.

While there, we prayed, we fasted, we talked, we laughed, we had the best time together.

Looking back now I see all the little moments God gave me along this journey.

It was the beginning of August when she had her follow-up appointment to see how the surgeries had helped.

They hadn't!

She was sent home, and hospice was called.

This didn't waver my faith at all. I knew that God had already healed her, and we were just waiting for the manifestation of the healing. It didn't matter what the doctors said; it mattered what Yahweh said in His word.

August 9th, my birthday, me, my husband Billy, and the kids headed up to Defuniak Springs to be with Mom and the entire family as hospice was there and saying Mom didn't have much longer to live.

My younger brother Ben and his fiancé moved their wedding date up to August 12th so that my mom could watch her baby boy get married and what a joy it was for her.

On August 13th, a little after noon, my mom stepped into eternity with a huge smile on her face and family surrounding her.

At that moment my world and faith shattered into a million little pieces.

For months after mom passed, I was so numb. If you've lost someone close to you, you know that feeling. You walk around almost in an out of body experience not knowing if you're coming or going. I remember standing at the gas pump and it was asking me for my zip code, and I couldn't remember it. I called my husband crying to ask him what our zip code was.

Billy and I spent that first Christmas without mom with my sister and her family in Virginia.

On the drive from Florida to Virginia, our van broke down not once, but twice. My sister and nephew had to come get us in North Carolina where we had to leave the van to get fixed. The transmission decided that it was time to kick the can.

After staying in Virginia a little longer than expected, we headed home nine days later.

While on the way home our van broke down *again*!

That was the straw that broke the proverbial camel's back.

It was in that moment that any fiber of hope and faith for me was gone. I couldn't believe or trust in a God that would take my mother from me and then allow our van to break down *three* times knowing we were in a financial struggle and didn't know where our next meal was coming from.

When we arrived home, I had already decided that this life was not worth living, that my children would be better off without me, that my husband could find someone else, and that family and friends in time would heal and move on.

The morning I chose to end it all, I told my husband that he should probably call his prayer warrior friends to pray to God because when he got home from work he wasn't going to have a wife anymore. It wasn't until recently that he shared with me, "The only way I could walk out the door that morning was because my faith wasn't in you or your words but in God and His words."

I remember being on my hands and knees scrubbing the hallway floor screaming out from the depths of my soul while tears were streaming down my face. The spirit of hopelessness was consuming me.

The meaning of hopelessness is a feeling or state of despair; lack of hope, having no expectation of good or success

In that moment I became painfully aware that my hope was fully vested in Yahweh and His word. My hope for each moment of the day. My hope for today. My hope for tomorrow. My hope for the future. It was all wrapped up in Yahweh. I trusted Him in everything, and He let me down.

Something clicked within me while I was scrubbing that floor. It was that still small voice of the Holy Spirit and I remember saying out loud, "Give it one more day Audrey and see what happens tomorrow."

The next day nothing big happened, but nothing bad happened either.

I can't really pinpoint when it was, but the Holy Spirit began revealing to me where I could find God in the midst of my storm.

I started to remember...

Psalm 77:11 tells us, "I will remember the deeds of the LORD; yes, I will remember your miracles of long ago. I will consider all your works and meditate on all your mighty deeds."

This is exactly what I started doing. I remembered all the different ways God had shown up for me.

The smile on my mom's face right before she took her last breath. Oh, if you could have seen it you would have known as we did she was seeing the face of Jesus Christ. God's presence was so tangible in that room when she went home to be with the Lord.

The day after she passed, my sisters and I went shopping for her Celebration of Life party and my sister's receipt was $43.43. My mom's birthday was April 3, 1943 (4/3/43). It had also stormed that morning, so when we were leaving the house, we witnessed the brightest rainbow that any of us had ever seen. To this day I've never witnessed a rainbow so distinct and vibrant with color.

I remembered those two times the van broke down on the way to Virginia, my brother Ray and my sister Rhonda were there to help us while my dad paid for the van to be fixed both times.

When the van broke down for the third time coming home from Virginia, our friends Melissa and Jim, who were in North Carolina visiting family for the holidays, were heading home too and were just thirty minutes behind us. They met us at the auto parts store and purchased the part we needed, helped put it in and followed us home.

I remembered that I was given six weeks with my mom that summer. Those were the most amazing days that God knew I needed for what was coming.

Those months following that day of almost ending it all were filled with memories and moments that kept reminding me of the faithfulness of God and His goodness towards me.

I became intimate with our heavenly Father like never before. I started reading my bible more than I ever had and not only did His truths start to be revealed but so did His character.

I learned that what we consider death is *not* death at all.

We are a spirit and have a soul which is our mind, will, and emotions. When this fleshly body gives way, our spirit and soul continue on. It doesn't die.

I didn't lose my mom to cancer. My mom's spirit and soul didn't die. She is in the land of the living where I will get to be with her for all eternity.

Just as one of my favorite books in the bible states, Ecclesiastes 3:1 "There is a season for everything, a time for every occupation under heaven: A time for giving birth and a time to die."

It's all in God's timing, His appointed and perfect timing.

I learned that the most powerful prayer you can ever pray is, "Abba, not my will but *your* will be done!"

I'll never forget the women in my homeschooling group praying for me and mom. One of the ladies said, "Nevertheless Lord, your will be done!"

She was alluding to the possibility that my mom would not be healed on this earth but that it was the Lord's will to take her home.

Now, remember, when that happened, I was standing with my mom in faith that God was going to heal her of cancer, and it was not her time to go home to be with Him.

So that prayer of "Thy will be done" to me was not said in faith and was a pretty weak prayer in my opinion.

Oh, how I was so wrong!

Over the years I've learned how powerful those four words are, "Thy will be done!"

You know they're powerful if Jesus prayed it *three* times in the garden of Gethsemane, "O My Abba, if it is possible, let this cup pass from Me; nevertheless, not as I will, but as You will." He knew what was coming and still prayed that prayer!

I found myself having to use that prayer six years later when I received a call from my older brother Ray telling me that he had just been diagnosed with colon cancer, stage 4, and they would be trying a new treatment on him.

It was Deja Vu all over again.

He wanted me to stand with him in faith and believe for a miracle. Of course I did, but this time I was keenly aware that God's will may not be to heal him here on this earth but in heaven.

I feel the need to stop right here and share something with you. The church I was going to at the time was all about the faith movement, the name it and claim it, the prosperity message. For me, I felt that even saying, "Lord, your will be done," at the end of my prayers was not having enough faith. It wasn't believing that God could do miracles. I felt like my prayers were so weak and that I was being double-minded.

The fact was my prayers were just getting stronger and more in tune to the Holy Spirit.

When my brother and I prayed together, we both understood that God had already healed him whether it be on this side of heaven or not. Not our will but Your will be done, Abba.

All of us siblings were together again, six years later, in August to spend time with my brother while he was in the hospital. When I left to head home, I told him that I expected to get a call telling me that he walked up out of that hospital room, healed and whole. Two days later on my fortieth birthday, my sister Melissa called to let me know that Ray was gone: he went home to be in Glory.

I just had to laugh because knowing my brother, he would have laughed at the fact that it happened on my birthday. This time though, I knew my prayers were answered because darn if he didn't get up out of that hospital room and walk out a healed man.

Do I miss my brother and our talks? You bet I do. To this day I still cry out of nowhere because I miss my mom and brother so much.

But God is right there to comfort me and remind me that it is just temporary and soon I'll be with them.

God's will is far greater than my will and your will, plus it's perfect in every way.

I learned to run to the Father first and foremost!

If I'm being honest, I ran to my mom for *everything*. I mean I would call her at least 3-5 times, and if a day went by where I didn't talk to her, I felt so lost.

With every financial blow Billy and I took, I would call her up crying my eyes out asking why God would allow all this stuff to keep happening to us.

With every situation I had with the kids, I would call her up asking for advice on how she thought I should handle it.

When I would get weary and done with homeschooling, she was the one to pick me back up, remind me why I was doing it, and then encourage me to keep on going.

When I had questions about God and His word, she would either answer them or send me in the direction I needed to go to find the answer.

I didn't realize how much I depended on my mom until she was no longer there.

Worse than that, I realized how much I didn't depend on nor run to the Father!

All throughout scripture God reminds us to come to Him first and foremost.

Jesus tells us in Matthew 11:28: "Come to me, all who are weary and burdened, and I will give you rest."

That's what I was truly seeking...rest from the cares of this world. Instead of running to mom, I should have been running to the feet of Jesus.

Again Proverbs 3:6 proclaims, "In everything you do, put God first, and he will direct you and crown your efforts with success."

God was my second choice. I wasn't truly putting Him first in everything. I was asking Him to direct my path but then just assumed that His direction would come through my mom.

Don't get me wrong, God used my mom on many occasions to speak to me, but I now know eighteen years later that my first response to anything is to fall at the feet of Jesus and seek His will first. Then if He chooses to use those in my life to speak to me, so be it.

I learned how to forgive God.

I always thought forgiveness was given to others and yourself. It never crossed my mind that I could feel betrayed by God and hold unforgiveness in my heart towards Him.

I'm no theologian or anything but isn't that like blasphemy or something. He is the one that gives forgiveness, not the other way around, right?

Well, when the Holy Spirit revealed to me that I was holding this unforgiveness in my heart towards Him because I felt betrayed, it was such a defining moment in my walk with Him.

I did feel like He betrayed me. In my heart, I had trusted Him and had 100% faith that He was going to heal my mom of cancer and bring us up out of our financial woes.

When the exact opposite of this happened, my trust was broken and faith shattered.

But I'm here to tell you, when I told the Lord, "I forgive you," that commandment of "Love the Lord your God with all your heart, soul, mind, and strength," flooded in and for the first time I understood what that meant.

I also learned that God did not betray me; I just never surrendered to His will.

I learned how to fully trust God in *all things*.

Proverbs 3:5-6: "Trust in the Lord with all your heart and lean not unto your own understanding. In *all* your ways, acknowledge Him and He will direct your path."

After Mom passed, Dad moved into a retirement home where he became the life of the party. He got himself a red convertible, something he always wanted, and traveled the United States. I spoke to him almost every single day, especially when he needed help with social media and his electronic devices.

It was in 2015 that Dad was diagnosed with prostate cancer. His mindset was unbelievable. I think after watching my mom and brother go through what they did, he decided that instead of chemo, radiation, and all the other drugs, his treatments would be to travel more and just live the life God gave him.

When it spread to his bones and he knew I was starting to get melancholy, he would always tell me, "Audrey Anna, death is just a part of life. You are going to be fine."

This time, I knew I would be okay because I had learned to run to my Abba Yahweh, where I found peace, joy, and comfort, even while watching my dad's physical body decline.

Did I pray for healing?

Absolutely! Our God is still in the business of performing miracles. I hear wonderful testimonies every day of people being supernaturally healed and experiencing financial breakthroughs.

But do you know the miracles I've come to recognize and experience even more deeply?

- It's the miracle of salvation and knowing where we get to spend eternity.

- It's the miracle of being able to have joy unspeakable in the sadness and calamity.

- It's the miracle of having peace that goes beyond all understanding in the midst of chaos.

- It's the miracle of watching someone's heart change completely towards God right before your eyes.

- It's the miracle of sitting in quiet and hearing that still small voice of Yahweh speak right to your heart through His word.

- It's the miracle of surrendering to God's will and knowing that it's always perfect... even when I don't see it or understand it.

- It's the miracle of forgiveness towards others, myself and God.

- It's the miracle of comfort while your heart is breaking in pieces.

December 9, 2022, Dad took his last breath on this earth and his first breath in eternity. The days leading up to that moment were filled with so much healing, laughter and tears.

I was in a totally new place with Yahweh this time around. I knew it was Dad's time to be in the presence of the Lord and instead of praying my will, I prayed God's will and boy did He show up.

A couple of hours before Dad passed, Yahweh gave me the opportunity to be alone with my dad. After joking with him and telling him that he better not pass while it's just me in the room, I prayed over the man that was my hero. I thanked the Lord for giving us kids such an amazing dad who raised us in the way of the Lord. Although he wasn't perfect, he was the perfect dad for us. I asked the Lord to not draw out the inevitable and to take Dad quickly and painlessly.

My older sisters got back from getting us lunch, so we went up on the rooftop to eat. When we were done, we came back to Dad's room. The nurse at the station right outside of his room was just sitting down from checking on Dad. She said he was doing good, but as we walked in the room, my sisters, who walked in first, knew right away that he must have just taken his final breath.

One of the things that Dad wanted more than anything was for none of us to be in the room when he took that final breath. Yahweh answered that prayer... and mine. Because it was only thirty minutes after I prayed that the Lord would take him quickly to his final destination to be home with our Abba Yahweh and my mom and brother.

1 Corinthians 15:55: "O death, where is thy sting? O grave, where is thy victory? The sting of death is sin; and the strength of sin is the law. But

thanks be to God, which giveth us the victory through our Lord Jesus Christ."

Oh, how I miss my mom, dad, and brother. There are days when grief hits me so hard I can't breathe, but then I am reminded of...

The miracle of hope.

Hope is more than just a feeling; it's an anchor for our souls. It's the assurance that no matter what we face, there is always something greater ahead. Even when the waves of life seem too strong, hope keeps us steady, reminding us that God is still in control.

We may not always understand His plans, and there will be moments when everything around us seems to crumble. But in those moments, when despair knocks at the door, hope reminds us that we are never alone.

There will be times when life feels too heavy, and the temptation to give up on hope feels real. But it's in those very moments that hope becomes our greatest strength. It's in the times of uncertainty that hope shines brightest, reminding us that what we see is not the end of the story.

God is working behind the scenes, weaving together every thread of our lives for His glory and our good, even if we can't see it now.

So, as you journey through life—through the valleys of loss, uncertainty, or hardship—hold tightly to hope. It will not disappoint. Hope is not a vague wish for better days, but a confident expectation, grounded in the truth of who Yahweh is. He is faithful, He is working, and He will never abandon you.

Never lose sight of hope, for it is the light that leads us home. It is the unbreakable promise that no matter how dark today may seem, the dawn is coming. And with it, the fullness of Yahweh's love and goodness.

And as long as there is hope, there is a reason to keep pressing forward.

Contact Information:
Audrey Ostoyic
SEO Expert and Serial Entrepreneur
www.audreyostoyic.com

She Laughs Without Fear of Her Health

A Journey of Faith, Family, and Fulfillment

Shontal LeJune

For as long as I can remember, my life has been a delicate dance between faith, family, and the pursuit of purpose. I didn't set out with a map in hand, but rather, a heart full of hope, curiosity, and a deep trust in God's plan for me. Little did I know that this journey would take me from the comforting rhythm of motherhood and homeschooling to discovering a passion for holistic living, home cooking, educating others, and embracing nature's gifts.

Early Journey of Faith and Purpose

Proverbs 3:5-6 (NKJV) - *Trust in the Lord with all your heart, And lean not on your own understanding; In all your ways acknowledge* Him, And He shall direct your paths.

This is not just a story about change, it's about growth, resilience, and the quiet strength that comes from nurturing what truly matters. Every step, every moment of doubt or joy, has been part of the larger tapestry woven by love, family, and faith. This is my story — and perhaps, it reflects your own.

It was this journey of nurturing what matters most that led me to discover the importance of holistic health. As I experienced the highs and lows of motherhood, I realized that true well-being involves more than just physical health. I'd like to start by explaining exactly what holistic health is. Holistic health is an approach to well-being that considers the whole person – mind, body, and spirit - in the pursuit of optimal health and wellness. Unlike conventional medicine, which often focuses on treating specific symptoms or illnesses, holistic health aims to understand the root cause of issues and promotes balance across all aspects of life.

My own journey into holistic health began after my first pregnancy when I started noticing changes in my body and mind. Initially, I attributed it to the natural shifts my body had undergone during pregnancy, coupled with the post-pregnancy hormone changes that often come with childbirth. After childbirth, I expected to bounce back; instead, I experienced a vast list of symptoms like chronic fatigue, digestive issues, mood swings, brain fog, heart palpitations, high anxiety, and more. At the time, I chalked it up to the natural adjustments of motherhood. While I expected my body to gradually recover, things did not seem to improve. I pushed through, as best as I could, assuming it was just the new normal of life after pregnancy and the beginning of motherhood, but deep down, I sensed something more was unfolding.

Then came my second pregnancy. After giving birth again, the issues that had initially seemed manageable became much more prominent. I found myself more exhausted than ever, my energy levels were at an all-time low, and my overall well-being felt off. The physical and mental symptoms were so much more pronounced, and I began to realize that this was not just the typical post-pregnancy experience. Something deeper was wrong, and I could not ignore it anymore.

Over the course of an eight-year period, starting shortly after my first pregnancy, I saw several doctors, determined to find answers. I underwent numerous tests – bloodwork, electrocardiograms (EKG), almost yearly thyroid testing, and imaging studies, like ultrasounds and upper gastrointestinal series to name a few, all hoping for a diagnosis or at least a direction to pursue. Time and time again, the results came back "within normal range", leaving me frustrated and absolutely confused. Despite my persistent symptoms, I was left without concrete answers or solutions, often hearing, "Everything looks fine." or, "You just have a little bit of a nervous stomach." Each visit felt like a dead end, and my health continued to fall out of balance, day after day, without any clear path forward.

As I continued to grapple with these overwhelming symptoms, I began to understand that my journey of healing was not just about addressing physical ailments but also about uncovering deeper layers of my well-being.

I knew that I could not be the only mom feeling these emotions and dealing with this level of stress after birth. I talked to everyone I knew, asking about their experiences, hoping for some sort of "light bulb" moment. There were so many other challenges like navigating the healthcare system, because "within normal range", does not always line up with how you feel physically, mentally, or emotionally.

During that time, I felt like I was slowly dying inside; as if a part of me was fading with each passing day. It wasn't just a fleeting tiredness, it was a bone-deep exhaustion that I could not shake no matter how much I rested nor how much I slept, when I did sleep. My energy was completely drained, leaving me feeling hollow and barely able to get through each day. Every time I ate, no matter what it was, my body responded with discomfort, as though my digestive system was rejecting everything I put into it. Meals, once a source of nourishment and pleasure, became moments of dread. Each meal brought on a heavy feeling in my stomach, along with bloating and nausea, turning the simple act of eating into a constant source of discomfort and anxiety. It was not just occasional; it was every single meal, every single day.

At this point, I was in my early thirties, supposedly in the prime of my life - when I should have felt strong, capable, and energetic enough to run around with my young children. But instead, it felt like my life was depleting before my own eyes. I could sense, deep down, that something was seriously wrong. My body was screaming at me with every symptom, every wave of fatigue, every moment of discomfort, that this was not normal. And yet, despite seeking help, I kept receiving answers that did not resonate with me. At one point, I really thought that maybe I had some rare form of disease that no one had discovered. Why else would I continue to go to doctors to only end up with no answers? They're supposed to be the experts, right? Where was my relief and solution? Maybe this was all stress from pregnancy, but geez, to this depth? I didn't realize that pregnancy would cause such havoc on one's body. It just couldn't be that this was how life was to go on. None of these explanations captured the depth of what I was experiencing. Everything from the doctors' mouths felt dismissive and incomplete. They truly were not hearing me. They couldn't be. Maybe I wasn't explaining clearly enough. There were so many questions I had when I would leave and there were so many tears.

Struggles and Perseverance

2 Corinthians 12:9 (NKJV) - But He said to me, 'My grace is sufficient for you, for My strength is made perfect in weakness.' Therefore most gladly I will rather boast in my infirmities, that the power of Christ may rest upon me.
Psalm 46:1 (NKJV) - *God is our refuge and strength, a very present help in trouble.*

I began to have thoughts that consisted of, '*How will my family get along without me if I find no resolve?*' '*Will my kids be ok if something happens to* me?' 'My sweet husband and best friend, how will life go on for him if something happens to me? How hard would life be for him raising two boys alone, all while trying to keep everything else afloat?" I tried so hard to stop thinking that way. To stop thinking about what life would be like in ten years if I was bedridden and couldn't be the mom or wife that I had dreamed of being for them. I wondered what would happen if the doctors continued to give no answers. Was there a way out for me? It got to be a pretty dark place at times. Somehow, through the grace of God, I seemed to continue to have a burning flame of persistence and determination to find out what was wrong with me. When these thoughts would come, there were many days when I told myself to get up and suck it up for their sake. It's what kept me going forward. Truly. Because the only way we can win when we get hit hard is to Keep. Moving. Forward.

So, I persisted, kept praying, kept pushing, and kept seeking, even though I felt like I was hitting walls at every turn. I turned inward, continually drawing on my faith as a source of strength. I continued to pray, not just for healing, but for clarity, guidance, and for help. I prayed for the wisdom to find the right path forward, for the patience to endure the process, and for the strength to keep showing up for myself; to look for answers, even when it didn't feel like I would get an answer. It became a very delicate balance not to lose what little sanity I felt I had left. I held onto the hope that I would somehow find the answers that I so desperately was searching for.

Finding Guidance and Healing

James 1:5 (NKJV) - *If any of you lacks wisdom, let him ask of God, who gives to all liberally and without reproach, and it will be given to him.*

Jeremiah 17:14 (NKJV) – *Heal me, O' Lord, and I shall be healed; Save me, and I shall be saved, For You are my praise.*

At a time when I was feeling lost and frustrated, and after a few years of focused prayer, God opened a door I hadn't even known was there. Through a thoughtful and considerate family member who was a local, natural pharmacist, this door led me to her coworker, who was also a natural pharmacist. A woman who, in a single conversation, would help me uncover the root cause of my suffering in less than an hour on a tearful phone call and shift me into what I call "phase one" of my holistic healing journey. I had never imagined that something so life-altering could come from an unexpected connection. It is truly amazing how God works. As I spoke to her, sharing the details of my story - the fatigue, the daily discomfort - I could sense a deep understanding in her responses, unlike any I had encountered before. Her compassion was felt so deeply.

Within this hour on the phone, she offered a diagnosis. I could hardly believe what I was hearing. After over eight years of seeing doctors and specialists, trying different treatments and self-help, and nearly giving up hope that anyone could pinpoint what was going on, there her answer was: Adrenal Fatigue. Adrenal fatigue is a condition where the adrenal glands, which produce stress hormones like cortisol, become overworked and depleted due to chronic stress. This can lead to symptoms such as extreme fatigue, difficulty waking up, body aches, and trouble coping with stress. It is a result of prolonged physical, emotional, or mental stress; in my case all three. This is a term I never heard from one conventional doctor I saw. I've come to learn that it's not something that is recognized much in the conventional world.

On the call, her words clicked into place, making sense of the symptoms I had been experiencing for so long. It was the first time someone had been able to give me a clear answer, and though it seemed almost too simple, I felt such a relief and a sense of peace; I knew it was God's hand that had moved. God had provided when I was at the end of my rope, as only He can do. It was a great reminder of His perfect design for His creation and growing even more in trusting Him with my future.

We moved forward with a simple saliva test to confirm the diagnosis, and when the results came back, they validated everything she had said. I remember feeling a mix of relief and disbelief. Finally, I had a name for what was happening inside my body. As I would come to learn, this was an additional layer atop several others barricading my complete healing. So, with this newfound clarity, she quickly set me up on a regimen of whole food supplements, specifically designed to support my adrenal health, along with some key lifestyle changes. She didn't treat me with a prescription, she guided me toward a more holistic way of living and a revolutionary answer. These changes lead to my first of many natural detoxes.

Within two months, I began noticing major shifts in my energy levels. It wasn't just about feeling better; I was starting to feel like myself again and it was a prayer answered. The constant brain fog and overall fatigue that had weighed me down for years was beginning to lift, and for the first time in so long, I felt hope returning. I wasn't just surviving each day, I was starting to thrive again. I remember my husband coming with me to this local pharmacy to get supplement refills and when he saw the holistic pharmacist, he said to her, "Thank you for giving me my wife back." I'll never forget that, and I'll never forget her humble smile in that moment. It's evident that our illness does not just affect ourselves; it affects our families just as deeply. I remember how hard it was to see the worry in my family's eyes as they watched me struggle with discomfort each day.

As I've learned through my health challenges, advocating for yourself is absolutely vital. No one knows your body, your mind, or your soul better than you. Trust in the inner wisdom that tells you when something isn't right, even if others don't understand it. It was through persistence and self-advocacy that I found the answers I needed to reclaim my health. As a health coach, I share my journey with others, helping them find their own path to wellness. I encourage them to ask important questions and to never settle for feeling anything less than their best. Remember, you have the power to advocate for your own health and happiness.

As I journeyed on, I embraced the lifestyle changes she recommended: cleaner eating, better sleep habits, and stress management techniques. I could see how these simple adjustments, combined with the supplements, were making a world of difference with each day that passed.

This moment in time radically changed my life and put me on a path I had never expected. It wasn't just about healing my body. It was about reclaiming my life, my energy, and my sense of purpose. I followed the regimen faithfully for nearly two years, and by then I had made such tremendous progress that I no longer thought I needed the supplements. I had reached a place where I felt healthier, more vibrant, and more in tune with my body than I had in years past. At the same time, I was still new to this holistic lifestyle and had yet to grasp its complete meaning.

Clarity and Answers to Health Issues

Jeremiah 33:6 (NKJV) - *Behold, I will bring it health and healing; I will heal them and reveal to them the abundance of peace and truth.*

Even though I had come so far in my health journey, I soon realized it was far from over. Little did I know that while my body had healed significantly, there were still deeper layers of growth and healing waiting to surface. These underlying issues hadn't fully revealed themselves during the early stages of recovery. As grateful as I was for the progress I had made, I became aware that there was still more work to be done — not just for my physical health, but for my mental, emotional, and spiritual well-being.

It was during this new phase, "phase 2", that I began integrating cognitive behavioral therapy (CBT) into my healing process. This is also a practice I continually keep at the forefront of my holistic toolbox. This approach was instrumental in addressing and reframing my thought patterns, which helped alleviate mental stress and contributed to my overall well-being. Through CBT, I was able to confront and process past traumas, creating space for deeper healing. This was a pivotal realization: to truly heal, both the mind, body, and spirit must be addressed, as they are profoundly interconnected.

Around this time, a new chapter of my journey opened up. My mom had been dealing with her own health issues, and we'd heard about a local holistic, chiropractic doctor who approached health in the way that I was introduced to through the holistic pharmacy. When my mom asked if I would walk alongside her in her health journey, I felt my body was telling me I needed something different also. I agreed to go with her, uncertain, but open to the possibility, because mostly, I felt like I was "ok", especially compared to where I had been a couple of years prior.

From the moment we began to be consulted by the doctor, our experience was more thorough than we had imagined. To begin, he conducted a full blood panel and a hair toxin analysis. These were tests I had never experienced or been offered with my previous conventional doctor during that eight-year period. The results were eye-opening, to say the least. It wasn't just one thing, it was a combination of underlying issues that had been affecting my health for many years prior. My blood work revealed imbalances, while the hair analysis detected toxins and heavy metals in my system that were also environmental. It all made sense and I started to realize that my lingering health issues weren't random, even though I had been feeling much better. It was all connected at a root level to how my body was functioning.

As we explored these findings further, I was also diagnosed with a couple of food intolerances. This was another turning point for me. I finally understood why I often experienced those pains after eating, even from back in childhood!

Discovering these intolerances was like finally uncovering a piece of my health puzzle that had been missing all my life. The foods I had been consuming without a second thought were actually contributing to years of inflammation and digestive issues. It was shocking and relieving at the same time. Once again I finally had more answers.

Overcoming Trials and Embracing New Changes

Matthew 11:28 (NKJV) - *Come to Me, all you who labor and are heavy laden, and I will give you rest.*

With this new knowledge in hand, I began the biggest and most pivotal detox process of my life to rid my body of built-up toxins, by cutting out sugar, wheat, and dairy. This wasn't just about taking supplements, or in conventional medicine, a prescription medication, and hoping for a quick fix; it was a long process. The detox, combined with the right supplements to support my system, made a world of difference. Slowly, but surely, my energy levels began to return at an even greater level than before, and I felt like I was reclaiming my health, on new levels, one step at a time. I started to feel lighter, not just physically but mentally. I started to feel more energized, my digestion improved, and my overall well-being flourished in ways I hadn't thought possible. I felt as if a huge weight had been lifted from my shoulders. Throughout this healing journey, I have learned just how important a quarterly detox is to rid our bodies of any build-ups we encounter, internally or environmentally.

But I'll be honest, this whole process required a level of discipline I hadn't known before. It wasn't just about changing my diet or taking new supplements, it was a complete shift in how I viewed my health. There's that lifestyle word again. I had to unlearn old habits and embrace new ones, and that took time. In fact, it took years of learning, understanding, and applying these newfound concepts. The path was challenging, but the rewards were undeniable!

Before starting my holistic journey, my view of healthcare was rooted in the conventional doctor's approach. I trusted that doctors knew best, and while conventional medicine has a vital role in diagnosing and treating diseases, I began to see its limitations. Conventional doctors are often focused on treating specific diagnoses, yet there's a gap in care for those of us who fall between 'healthy' and 'ill.' When my own symptoms were vague and answers were scarce, I found myself in that frustrating gap, uncertain of what to do next.

The difference with the holistic, functional medicine approach is that it dives deeper, tracing issues back to their root causes. It does not just treat the surface-level symptoms but looks at the body as an interconnected system. This approach does not offer a quick fix, but it does offer a solution that promotes healing over time, with patience. My body was responding, and my health was transforming.

Embracing Knowledge and Continuing the Journey

Proverbs 2:6 (NKJV) - *For the Lord gives wisdom; From His mouth come knowledge and understanding.*

After another couple of years passed, phase three of my journey into holistic health and wellness began. I found myself in a completely new place in my life, mentally, physically, and spiritually, fully immersed in a world I never imagined I would be a part of. I devoured books on natural healing from some of the best authors in the field, diving deep into research on supplements, and exploring all things holistic. A total nerd, right? What started as a personal quest to heal had become a full-blown passion. I was constantly joining online health summits, listening to countless podcasts, and following the wisdom of leading holistic health gurus in every spare moment I had. The knowledge I was gaining was vast, and every new insight felt like another piece of the puzzle falling into place.

As I soaked in all this information, my love for functional medicine grew exponentially. It wasn't just about my personal healing anymore. It radically changed my life, and I began witnessing firsthand how it was changing the lives of people around me as I shared my journey and experiences. Friends, family, and even acquaintances were benefiting from the insights I had gained. I became almost like a health detective, constantly on the lookout for answers for them, and I was able to direct them toward solutions that worked for them. It was a decade of transformation, both for myself and for those who crossed my path during that time.

In 2022, I decided it was time to take this passion to the next level. I enrolled at the Institute for Integrative Nutrition (IIN), eager to formalize the knowledge I had been gathering. The decision to attend IIN felt like a natural evolution of everything I had learned over the years. I've always been fascinated by the science behind holistic health, understanding the intricacies of the body and how everything works together in harmony. I became even more engrossed in the field, particularly loving how holistic practices incorporated science with the wisdom of nature and what God created. I was so excited to be a part of this educational journey that I also completed the Whole Person Health course through IIN, earning another certification and deepening my understanding of how to care for the body as a complete system.

But my hunger for knowledge didn't stop there. I continued reading, researching, and listening to podcasts, and I have plans for more educational classes because frankly, I just can't get enough. Every new piece of information feeds my passion and motivates me to learn more.

My fifteen-year journey was more than just gathering information — it was about personal experience, learning through trial and error, and discovering life's lessons firsthand. My health struggles, extensive research, formal education, and real-world application have equipped me to advocate fiercely for myself, my family, and others, always striving for deeper, more fulfilling answers in health.

My mission is to promote the vital importance of functional, holistic living in a world that often overlooks it. Life is meant to be lived fully, with intention and alignment to our design. As an Integrative Nutrition Health Coach, I am passionate about empowering women to advocate for themselves and their families, through practical, personalized solutions addressing their mental, physical, and spiritual, well-being. Through education, coaching, and accessible tools, I guide others to take control of their health in ways that feel achievable and empowering. Together, we can return to the simplicity and abundance that God intended for us, one step at a time, deeply grounding us to the One who created us.

Reflecting on Creation and Divine Design

Genesis 1:31 (NKJV) - *Then God saw everything that He had made, and indeed it was very good...*

In reflecting on what I've learned, I often return to a powerful thought that has grounded me through it all. As I take a breath, close my eyes, and envision God's Presence at the center of the Garden of Eden, a vivid image emerges: the lush greenery, the vibrant plants yielding whole, nourishing foods, the pure beauty of nature in perfect alignment. I picture the gentle movement of the wind, the stillness of the atmosphere, and the serenity that filled every corner. God, in His wisdom, created not only a place of abundance and provision, but a space for deep connection. Connection to Him, to the earth, and to ourselves. In this place, I feel the intentionality behind each element: the simplicity, the slowness of life, the meaningful movement that naturally occurred as Adam and Eve tended to the garden. There was no rush, no chaos, just the peaceful rhythm of creation. In that space, there was perfect provision for overall health: mentally, physically, and spiritually. I believe God designed it this way, not just for Adam and Eve, who dwelled in Eden, but as a model for us to draw from to restore our souls daily; to realign with the fundamental truths that sustain us.

This thought serves as my lifeline, a constant reminder in the fast-paced, chaotic world we live in. It calls me back to these timeless and foundational practices that stabilize, nourish, and ground me in everything I do. These principles: slowness, connection, whole foods, meaningful movement, and spiritual alignment are vital to the restoration of my soul. Every day, they help me maintain balance and wholeness. I believe that even in our modern world, we can imitate these principles to the best of our ability, incorporating them into our unique paths, to encourage a deeper sense of peace and overall well-being. This journey of faith, family, and fulfillment is shaped by patience, resilience, and hope, growing within each of us.

Contact Information:
Shontal LeJune
Integrative Nutrition Health Coach
www.SunshineLiving.com

My Oasis

Renee Kelley

I laugh in the face of fear!

I truly do laugh at my future!

I laugh at my future because there were times I could not see that I had a future. When I laugh, it is because God has the final say. I am laughing in the face of the enemy. I am laughing in the face of those that thought I would never make it. I am still here, and some of them are gone. Who do men think they are? I mean mankind. In the face of an almighty God, who do they think they are to hold my future? I laugh because there was a time in which all I could do was cry. I stand in a place now of great strength for I am victorious and no longer a victim.

There have been times when I didn't know if I would live to see another day. So many times, I wondered if I would see my next birthday.

My children now are grown and have children of their own. There was a time I did not know if I would live to see them out of school and of age. It was a struggle to bring them into this world, and then it was a struggle for me to live and to raise them. I raised them hard just in case they would have to take care of themselves at a young age. My husband did his best to take care of us all and he tried his best to be understanding. I was very sick and had more bad days than good. Sometimes it felt like a struggle just to breathe in and breathe out. No one outside the home truly knew my greatest challenges. It was, for the most part, a well-kept secret. So many times I was so feeble and weak in the natural, it would take days of rest before I could even leave home. I would go to church on Sunday like normal, while behind the scenes it would empty my small pool of energy. All would seem fine to the outside world. I had to rest for days before I could even do regular functions to keep my household running. I stood in a place of uncertainty with the enemy's voice lying and telling me I would die at a young age. He was whispering in my ear, *"You will be bedridden before you pass and will be of no real use to anyone."* So many times, I felt I was a burden instead of a blessing to my husband and my children. It is hard to admit, but I was raising my children to end up having a stepmother before they reached adulthood. I was confident I had done the right thing in preparing them for life. It was tearing me apart to know I would not be around to see their life truly play out. I began to believe the report of the deceptive lies of the enemy. I thank the Lord for those who stood in the gap when I could not hold my head up and pray for myself.

I want to share with all who will read these words.

The devil is a liar.

My future is bright, and I shall live until I die. I am with the living, therefore I will enjoy navigating through this journey called life.

"She laughs in the face of fear" has been heavy on my heart, for I have surely faced trials that were seemingly going to wipe me out. The events of life were like the big waves of the ocean as they came crashing down all around me.

At an early age, I was diagnosed with Fibromyalgia and chronic fatigue syndrome. I, at times, would be in so much pain I could not stand a soft sheet on my body. Later I was diagnosed with an autoimmune disorder that would bottom out my blood pressure to near death. It also would take my blood sugar to dangerous levels. I could not get one thing fixed or stable before I was faced with another devastating blow. At an even earlier age, I was uncertain at one point if I would have use of my limbs. I did find out later it was not a spinal injury, as the doctors had previously thought, but a vertebra in my neck and another in my lower back pinching nerves.

These two combined would cause paralysis and, at times, I could not walk. I also lost use of my right hand and arm and sometimes both arms and hands. I began to have anxiety attacks that would feel as though I was having a heart attack or stroke. It affected my blood and oxygen flow. I had to learn to breathe through the struggles and stress of life.

I also faced a time when I experienced what PTS (Post Traumatic Stress) truly felt like. I faced this challenge when my son literally was dying in my arms after a severe allergic reaction. But I cried out to God, and He heard my prayers! He brought life back to my son. Thank you, Jesus!

In my current season of life, He has set me free from severe anxiety and the posttraumatic effects. He has brought my body to a place where I do not suffer unbearable pain at a constant unbearable level. There is so much the Lord has brought me through.

During all those rough times, God truly sustained me. He helped me get my footing and laugh in the face of the enemy and his lies. I survived and survived again. Truly I will live until God carries me home. I am claiming the truth that I am not stuck in the middle; no in-between. I have been raised up from near death. I have overcome great obstacles that others have not survived. And I am living proof that you can as well.

Through Christ all things are possible.

"I can do all things through Christ which strengthens me." Philippians 4:13 KJV

"Jesus said unto him, if thou canst believe, all things are possible to him that believeth." Mark 9:23 KJV

You can. You CAN! YOU CAN!

It is hard to sum up all of what God has done for me in my lifetime. I have truly seen miracle after miracle in my life, my family's life, and the lives of many all around me. I have faced trial after trial and yet I am still standing.

Let me share with you a glimpse into my life and show you how I am able to laugh at my future!

Have you ever been standing where you feel you are standing alone? Many had spoken out against me, lied, and tried to slander my name. Yet God dealt with me to pray for His mercy and not His wrath for those who had stabbed me in the back.

As I began to pick myself up, I looked around and felt so alone. And yet He sent me to my Oasis – the place where it's just me and Him – in the midst of my desert place. There were those in that place who encouraged, strengthened, and lifted me up during my time of great sorrow. And then I began to praise Him in the storm. I praised Him in the midst of this great trial: the hardest things I had ever been through. I sought Him. I cried out to Him. I began to find myself longing to still away and pray. I began to thirst for a time of praise and worship, even if it was right by myself. In my own place and my own space, I began to find the refreshing. When I would go to my Oasis, I drank even more from the living water of life.

When I was among many, it didn't matter if no one else was worshiping. I truly did not care if I was the only one. I was not looking for satisfaction or justification or confirmation from others. It did not bother me if I was the loudest one in the crowd. I began to feel strength and comfort. I felt peace in the midst of this great trial. I am here to say you can stand, even if it feels like you are standing all alone.

I remember the worst day of my life becoming the best day of my life. I was in a terrible relationship. We were both young and dumb. It was a bittersweet five years in total. It ended abruptly and I thought my world was caving in all around me. Some days I felt like I could barely tread water, as the waves of life crashed in all around me. Yet soon there came a time where I found the ground began to solidify and I began to walk on water. No matter how the storm raged I had found my calm. God had truly come to my rescue, and He had given me my Oasis in the midst of my desert land.

As I reflect, that worst day of separation from someone I thought I would be with forever and be my one and only true love, turned into the best day because it was what led me to truly experience the depths of God's love for me.

I found myself drawing closer to the rock of my salvation. Prior to this experience I just thought I knew the Lord.

But through these rough lonely times, I realized I was truly never alone. I was still standing through it all. God had placed in my life the one He had ordained for my life. The one who He had picked out and chosen to walk beside me and work with me and help me; and also for me to be this for him through this journey of life. He truly was a God-send and a gift from God. We have been through the thick and the thin and yet God has kept us.

After that time of growth in the Lord, there came a time in the worst phases of my sickness when the doctors wanted to take my driver's license. They spoke over me, "There are some who are not in as bad of shape as you are, and yet they are bedridden with the same things you have been diagnosed with."

I refused to believe the report of the doctors. I chose to believe the report of the Lord, for He said in His word:

"Beloved, I wish above all things that thou mayest prosper and be in health, even as thy soul prospereth." 3 John 1:2 KJV

I was standing on His promise, for I knew Jesus shed his blood on the cross for all our sins, and by his stripes, we are healed.

"Surely he hath borne our griefs, and carried our sorrows: yet we did esteem him stricken, smitten of God, and afflicted. But he was wounded for our transgressions, he was bruised for our iniquities: the chastisement of our peace was upon him; and with his stripes we are healed." Isaiah 53:4-5 KJV

I remember getting a call from a doctor on one particular weekend many years ago. I could hear the desperation and panic in her voice. Her tone was one of genuine concern for my well-being as she began to tell me the latest findings from my last test.

I began to laugh at her and I told her I did not receive that report.

She was very distraught and anger rose up within her voice as she said, "You need to take this seriously."

I then realized and found myself reassuring her. "I will do all I know to do and will trust the Lord with the rest."

At the time I was out of town at a camp meeting in North Carolina. I told her, "When I return home, I will do what you said is necessary." As I finished the conversation, I told her once more, "I know I am in God's hands. Thank you for calling me."

Many times, I have been prayed for, and after there would be a change for a time, but it seemed I had a hard time holding on to my healing. The best way to describe it was like a chiropractic adjustment. I would be better and then these afflictions would return. But I can say this, "Never be ashamed to get prayed for again." I would lay hands on myself and get some relief. My husband would pray and a change for a time would come.

Throughout the years I began to say "Lord, if you are not going to give me a miracle, then give me wisdom in what I must do for divine wisdom." I knew with wisdom my healing would come. I can not tell you how. I just knew it was something I had to walk out. We truly must do all we know to do to be in better health and prosper. I was willing to do my part.

I have learned in this journey called life that it is vitally important to surround yourself with those of like faith and believers in Christ. So many people have prayed for me consistently and they have been my village. We certainly must always remember we have need of one another. I have come a long way. I have overcome great odds and yet am still standing. I still am faced with challenges that are bigger than me, but they will never be bigger than the God we serve. Because of all the things I have faced, I have learned to enjoy the journey and not just the destination. I enjoy my children so much more now and my grandchildren as well. I realize life is not perfect nor are we perfect. There was only one perfect one and He died on the cross for all of us. We have a choice to choose Him as our Lord and Savior. He chose us first a long time ago.

The things that used to stress me out don't bother me as much anymore. The things I thought must be done in a day, I now realize: what is not done today can be done tomorrow, if tomorrow comes. I do squeeze the good out of a day and enjoy the day like there may possibly be no other. I set goals and have timelines to meet like everyone else. I just schedule in fun and rest all along the way. Stopping to smell the roses, so to speak. I rejoice in the small wins. If I am vertical and out of the bed moving, which most days I am, it is a good day.

We put too much undue stress upon ourselves, putting unrealistic goals and expectations in our own lives and those surrounding us. I am striving to accept the things I can not change. This has been a huge milestone for me. We must understand we are of value and our life is not our own. We must cherish the ones we love and certainly learn to love ourselves.
My testimony is this.

I stand here today driving the biggest vehicle I have ever owned and I have never had my license taken away from me. I walked through the time of having to be driven everywhere. But that season passed. Thank you, Jesus!

So many times, in my lifetime the enemy thought he had won. I laugh at the future because I know who holds my world in the palm of His hand. He holds my today and my tomorrow, for my God is well able to do exceedingly abundantly above all that I can ask or ever think.

"Now unto him that is able to do exceeding abundantly above all that we ask or think, according to the power that worketh in us," Ephesians 3:20 KJV

The discouragement comes when we think we know everything that we are supposed to do in our lifetime. We think we know what our today holds. We think, *'It is my life. I can live it like I want to.'*

But there is a peace that surpasses all understanding in knowing that we belong to him. He spoke us into existence and one day He will call us home to be with Him. The only way you can truly laugh at your future and know that everything will be alright is if you belong to Him. Make sure that you have accepted Jesus Christ as your savior. Make sure that you have repented and made things right with Him. Make sure you have been born of water and the Spirit. Make sure beyond a shadow of a doubt you are filled with His Spirit overflowing. Listen to His voice.

For God is able to supply all your needs according to His riches in glory.

"But my God shall supply all your need according to His riches in glory by Christ Jesus." Philippians 4:19 KJV

Allow the Spirit of God to lead you into all truth during this era where people do not believe you can be filled with the Holy Ghost. They think in this dispensation of time it no longer exists. Some think it has never existed. (A topic for another time).

I am here alive and well to tell you miracles have *not* ceased. The gifts of God are still flowing in the lives of His chosen seed. And yes, you can still be filled with the Holy Ghost. Speaking in tongues and Him speaking to you and through you is still happening today. I don't want to blow someone out of the water. But know this: when you accept Jesus Christ as your savior is not the moment when you are automatically filled with His Spirit. An infilling of the Holy Ghost is a gift and tongues have not ceased.

Some today may be hearing this for the very first time. It is your beginning into more of the deep things of God.

You may have been walking with God possibly even for a long time, doing all you knew to do. But now God is revealing more of His truths to you. It is okay, for we all may have come from different walks of life.

God would have us all to know Him in the fullness of who He really is. So therefore we all must start somewhere.

Just don't stop. We are ever learning and striving to know more and more about our Creator and Savior.

So, come on into the water. Wade on out into the deep. Stop being satisfied with what you have and where you stand. As you look down, you may realize you are in the shallow waters. But look up, for all that He has is available to those who seek Him with their whole heart.
I have come too far for anyone to be able to convince me that God is not real or to try and tell me He no longer works in the miraculous.

There are many times I have been through the test of life. I felt the fire raging all around me. But my God has always delivered me out of all my troubles.

"The righteous cry, and the LORD heareth, And delivereth them out of all their troubles." Psalm 34:17 KJV

Hear his voice. Speak to His ear!

He is ever speaking. We must be ever listening. He also is ever listening. Call out to Him and know you too can laugh at your future, because whatever others have thought about you or said you would never do, He will come through for you. Where others have spoken out against you and your enemies have left you for dead, God says, "You shall live and not die. You shall succeed and not fail. You shall learn to enjoy life and no longer be sad. You shall own your possessions and possess them, and they will not possess you." Money and things will no longer be what brings you happiness and fulfillment. You shall have joy and peace and be full of His glory.

Rest in Jesus, my dear sisters and brothers in Christ, for His peace truly does surpass all understanding. Let him be your Oasis and you too can laugh at your future. When the enemy says you are done, God says you have only just begun.

From my tablet to yours, learn to enjoy the journey!

Contact Information:
Sis Renee Kelley
Renee Kelley Endeavors LLC
Renee Kelley

God's Strength Through Life's Challenges

Karen Powers

My journey has always been very busy, but full of many blessings along the way. I have four great children: three boys and one girl. I have one beautiful granddaughter and a grandson on the way. I grew a whole new heart once I became a grandmother. My children have always been my greatest blessings from God. They have been my source of strength, encouragement, and love in life. I love to see them happy and enjoying their lives. I have also been blessed to have taught many wonderful children for thirty-two years – blessed to teach them and watch them grow and overcome their own challenges. For the last fifteen years, I have also been a private teacher to one very special little boy, who has had many health challenges and disabilities since he was born. He has been a total inspiration to me.

As I'm sure you know, life gets in the way sometimes, and we all face challenges and difficult circumstances along the way. I definitely had my fair share of these in life. My journey to become a health coach started after facing many health challenges for a long time. Sometimes you just don't understand why you go through certain things in life, but now I know. This story is about strength and how God has been there all along for me, but it took me so long to realize that and have faith in Him. God was my source of strength when I had to face all the difficult circumstances in my life, I have learned that I am stronger than I ever thought I was.

As a young child, I had a normal childhood and grew up with a great loving family. I was the oldest of three siblings. I have two brothers. We went on vacation and had big holiday parties with aunts, uncles, and cousins. Those were the days! My parents always made sure we did well in school. I had many friends to hang out with and have sleepovers and other things. My brothers and I went to Sunday School every Sunday. That was the beginning of my faith. After completing our confirmation - a sacrament in which a person strengthens their faith and commits to following Jesus Christ - we only went to church for holidays or on occasion, and my faith drifted away after that. On a different note, I had always seemed to get strep throat throughout my childhood. This continued way into my adulthood as well and created havoc in my body for a long time.

A few years later, I graduated high school and went on to college to become an elementary school teacher. I married at only twenty-one years old and had my first son at age twenty-four. I worked part-time as a teacher. My husband worked as a landscaper. I had my second son at twenty-six years old. I continued to work part-time when I could as finances were always tight. Life was getting busier with two little boys while working. I had always been a hard worker, and I just wanted to be a good mother to my children at the same time. That was very important to me. I would do whatever I needed for my children and my family: work, take care of them, go to doctor appointments, attend playdates, make dinner, clean, and all the other errands and responsibilities that go along with being a mother. I had the mindset that I always had to get everything done which eventually led to burnout. Can you relate?

Fourteen months later I had my third son at the age of twenty-eight. Life became even busier. I had one in preschool, and the other two were very close in age, always on the run. Thank goodness my parents and my in-laws were around to help babysit when needed. I was very grateful for that. They helped us out so much. Three years later, I had my fourth child, my daughter, at the age of thirty-one. I somehow had this never-ending strength to do all the physically demanding tasks of being a mother to four children, and I never knew where it came from. There wasn't any time to think about anything else. I was doing all that was given to me. As mom's, we just go, go, go and get things done, right?

A couple of years later, I decided to continue my education and go for my Master's Degree in Special Education. I had never actually wanted to be a Special Education teacher. I thought I wouldn't be able to do or handle that. But a special education teacher walked into my classroom one day and told me about what she did, and I was inspired and motivated to investigate it. She was there and worked one to one with a student of mine that was having difficulties.

They say people come into your life for a reason. I totally believe in that. I enrolled in the Master's Program at the same college where I received my Elementary Teacher Certification. I attended school in the evenings so my husband could stay home with the children. It took two years. My children were able to go to my graduation and watch me achieve this accomplishment I continued to show them you can do anything you put your mind to. This degree gave me more opportunities for a better job to support my family and start the career I was meant to go on. During this time, my husband worked a lot and was hardly home.

As my children grew up, the worries started as they became more independent. They started to hang out with their friends more, started driving, getting their first jobs and not being home as much as they used to. Just the normal part of growing up. I knew we raised them well, but as a parent, you still worry. It was at this time I had allowed fear to come in. It wasn't until then that I started to pray more, and I restarted my faith. As my children went through some difficult challenges in their adolescent years, I would lie awake at night going over decisions we had made, questioning myself if we missed anything. *"Did we do the right thing?"* I often asked.

Parenting does not come with a book on what to do. Arguments happened about how to handle our children's struggles. Hope and disappointment came in different waves. There were a lot of ups and downs. I started to pray to God that he would protect and guide them. A mother will do anything for her children. I certainly gave my all. Back then, I felt like my faith wasn't strong, but I continued to try and pray. I really didn't even know how to pray. Prayer wasn't really part of our lives after their religion classes were done. Of course, we went to church on occasions like a holiday or special family events, but it wasn't really talked about much or a "go-to" in our lives.

The time came to apply for a few teaching jobs. My first teaching job was at a Board of Cooperative Educational Services (BOCES) teaching adults. Then I became a preschool teacher and had my own classroom. This helped because my youngest child could come to work with me, and we didn't need a babysitter as much. In the evenings I tutored children in reading and math for extra money. I also was a substitute teacher in our local school district.

Eventually, I got a job as a special education teacher. This changed my life. It has been the most rewarding job to see what a difference you can make in a child's life, especially children with severe disabilities, diagnoses and other life conditions. This was the path I was meant to go on in my career and I believe it was a blessing given to me. It was an example of how God was working behind the scenes. I felt my faith growing; I was so grateful. I began to teach many, many children with different needs and disabilities. I have met wonderful, supportive families along the way. I started to get recommended by others to be their child's teacher.

Everything was going great. I was working full-time, and all my children were in school. Sports, Cub Scouts, Girl Scouts, homework, projects, many broken bones, surgeries, doctor appointments, orthodontic appointments, and driving my kids around were part of each day. My husband helped when he could. We were on the run always.

This was a turning point in my life. When I turned thirty-five, I was working in a school. I remember it was around Christmas time. I started to feel sick with a sore throat. I had always gotten strep throat throughout my life and figured it was just that again. Back then my doctors did not believe in getting my tonsils out. It was a busy time of year with work and my home life. There were lots of activities, holiday parties, and running around to do. It was a lot, but I put myself again on the back burner and thought, '*I will get to the doctor soon if I continue to feel terrible.*'

Well, I proceeded to get worse. I developed a rash, a high fever, and had bilateral joint pain starting from my ankles and slowly heading up to my shoulders over a week or two. I had no energy at all. My body was in a state of inflammation that I didn't even know about. I could actually feel the joint pain moving up through my body. I was not even able to walk. It was a very scary time.

I went to the emergency room and waited seven hours in a hallway for them to tell me it was just a virus. I thought to myself, "*Ok, it is just a virus. It will get better soon.*" My family watched me as I lay on the couch feeling so sick. I wasn't able to even get up, so I scooted on my bottom. My family knew when mom was down, there was something very wrong. They weren't used to seeing me that way. I couldn't go back to work. I was scared I would lose my job. I had all of these thoughts going through my head.

I set up an appointment with my primary doctor because I wasn't getting better, and he also said, "It is a virus. Give it some more time." Well three months later, after going back to the emergency room again, I was still being told it was a virus. All of my bloodwork and tests kept coming back normal. I knew something wasn't right at this point. I wasn't going to stop until I found the right answer. I was not getting better. I began to turn to God and pray for an answer. I knew it wasn't a virus. I persisted and was determined to find out what was really going on. I saw every kind of doctor to rule things out. Finally, after seeing a rheumatologist, I was diagnosed with rheumatic fever (strep throat related) and was sent to an infectious disease doctor to be treated with antibiotics for five years. Yes, five *years*.

At last, I was feeling better and went back to work full-time. This doctor did extensive testing on me. This rheumatologist was the answer God sent to me. That was a very stressful time in my life.

 I was so grateful for him, and I thanked God for this wonderful doctor. I had lost faith in other doctors out there. I thought to myself, *"This is who we have in charge of our health!"* I even changed primary doctors. Even after the five-year treatment, I continued to see the rheumatologist every six months for twenty years until he retired. He was the only doctor I trusted at that point.

There were always stressors in my life from being a very busy working mom: financial issues, marital issues that caused a lot of tension in our home, and unpredictable behaviors. but I continued to do what I had to do for my family and for what I thought was good for them. The constant stress left me feeling drained and overwhelmed. Who doesn't have any stress in their life? No one I know.

As parents, we always made sure the children could do whatever they asked to do such as buying certain clothes, going to the movies, signing up for different sports, etc. We wanted them to have a normal, fun childhood. As a family, we went on a few vacations over the years. We ate out a lot and got fast food because that was what the kids enjoyed. Healthy eating, what is that? During those times, I did not take time for myself at all, thinking that one day I would have time to do that stuff. I felt like I had no choice. *'God is going to get me through this. After all, he has blessed me in so many ways so far.'* My faith began to grow even more.

Five years later, my life changed forever. Not only did my father get diagnosed with cancer and was told he had three months to live, but around the same time that year, I became ill with two symptoms of an autoimmune disease. I had nystagmus and vertigo. It was another scary time. I thought, "Where *did this come from now?*" I headed back to the doctors to figure out what was going on with me.

After many, many tests, I was told I had a chronic condition which, "I would have for the rest of my life." The thought of being put on medication for the rest of my life was beyond stressful and frightening. It is not something I wanted to do. There had to be a different way. It led to feelings of uncertainty and frustration that comes with not knowing how your body will be from day to day. And I thought I was stressed before!

As always, I was determined to do what I had to do: get back to work and take care of the family. I was not going to give up. "I will get through this," I told myself. I prayed to God for healing for my father and myself. Soon after, my brother found an amazing surgeon for my father in NYC, and we believed this doctor was heaven-sent as he saved and prolonged my father's life. I thanked God for this. This was when I started to turn to God daily and pray for my father, myself, my family, and my children. My father lived for seven more years. His death took a big toll on me, and I still cry from time to time when I think of him. He was such a great man. I now believe that through prayer, we can hold on to hope and find the answers we need. This was one turning point in my life.

After that difficult time in my life, I started to seek God in everything I do. I started to pray every day for wisdom, knowledge, guidance, and protection to help me know what to do with my health as well as with watching over my family. Each day I woke up, I started to thank God for another day and for all the blessings and gifts He has given to me and my family over the years. I haven't missed a day of praying since. I know God will guide me to what I need and to my purpose. And He did.

I started to research a lot, looking for other ways to nourish my body rather than taking medication for the rest of my life. I joined several nutrition and autoimmune groups, read lots of books and other information on autoimmune conditions. I practiced deep breathing with an amazing person in an autoimmune group I belonged too. I met some great women going through similar situations that taught me about nourishing your body and lifestyle changes. I was on a mission. I learned about eating clean. I was determined to keep inflammation down in my body. I cut out many foods like dairy, sugar, gluten, soy, etc. I worked on stress management as stress has affected my health thus far. I started to cook healthy meals for my family. I started to exercise more. I did everything I could to stay strong and move forward without letting my health affect my children.

My children picked up on the healthier way of eating as I lived it out. I love to see them making healthy choices. I am still working my full-time job as a special education teacher, but this passion grew inside of me to look further, and I wanted to educate others about healthy living. Finally, I became a health coach after a year of schooling at the Institute of Integrative Nutrition (IIN). It was a great eye-opening experience, and I am so happy that I did it. I want to be able to share with others and my family how to get healthy and change their lifestyle so they can feel their best.

There have been bumps along the way, like two major unexpected colon surgeries within the last year, which was an extreme test of my faith. I couldn't believe this was happening again. God gave me strength once again to get through that difficult time. It was the most difficult health challenge yet. I was out of work for between three and four months and it took almost a whole year to get my strength back. It was a setback, but I didn't let it stop me. Sometimes the worst things in your life can be a blessing at the same time. I was grateful that I had started to take care of my health before all of this, otherwise it could have been worse.

Through my research and recovery, my journey continued as I learned about taking care of my body. I decided it was time to take care of myself. I had always put others first, which had been very important to me, but I also began to understand that God wanted me to take care of my body. My family needed me, so I decided to do everything possible to keep myself stable and live a long life. This became a passion of mine. I learned so much about food, nutrition and deep breathing. Over the last five to seven years, I have fully changed my lifestyle, full of determination.

I've learned to express my faith with greater boldness and less fear, after seeing all that God has done in my life. I now share more openly about prayer with my children and others in my life. My children will ask me to pray for them when they face difficult life challenges, and I always believe their prayers will be answered, even if not right away. We go through challenges and difficult circumstances so God can lead us onto the path He has chosen for us. It took a long time for me to realize this.

As my journey goes on, I am more prepared for the future. I pray morning, night, and whenever needed during the day. I had allowed fear to take over my life when all I needed was faith and to trust that everything would be okay. God has answered so many of my prayers. I am so thankful in so many ways. Even though I still fear at times, my faith is stronger than it ever has been. I have gotten through some really rough times. There will always be stress in our lives, but I am working on stopping the fear and anxious thoughts that come up by turning to prayer. It is because of the things that cause the most worry deep inside of me that I need daily reminders of strength, trust, and faith.

If you ask anyone who knows me, I am always smiling and willing to help others. You would never know what I have been through. My mission is now to help others learn the power of lifestyle habits and the significant shifts these can have on improving your health, relationships, finances, spiritual health, mindset, stress levels, boundaries and joy. Life is busy; however, we need to take care of the body that God has given us. We can heal our bodies. Everything happens for a reason so keep moving forward and never give up.

God is good.

Contact Information:
Karen Powers
Holistic Health Coach
www.simplywholeistic.com

Mountains Before Me

Denise LeDoux Leiato

Life is messy. There can be many "bumps" along that road, things that we don't expect or understand. God can, however, reduce these "bumps" or even "mountains" to plains, according to His Word. Zechariah 4:7 says, "What are you, mighty mountain? Before Zerubbabel, you will become level ground..." And in the previous verse, the Lord said to Zerubbabel, "Not by might, nor by power, but by my Spirit." And so, my friend, if you are facing a bump or mountain in your life today, have no despair, for God is no respecter of persons; what He has done for me, He can do for you! Come with me and see how God flattened mountains into plains.

I was in love with love, married to a nice guy but the wrong guy. I made him and myself miserable. We lived our separate lives, then separated; we got back together and found ourselves pregnant. I had an incompetent cervix, which meant it thinned out and could no longer hold the pregnancy. I delivered too early and lost a beautiful baby girl named Anna Maria whose lungs were not developed. So I had to deal with the first mountain: the mountain of Death. We had a funeral with a little pink casket.

It was a very painful time, a dark period, as I tried to be the "good Christian woman". I thought I had to pop back to normal very joyfully. I pushed my grief deep down inside, not dealing with it. This was very dangerous because stuffing emotions causes them to erupt at inopportune times.

One such time was during the next Christmas holiday, when I had difficulty being around nieces and nephews. I suffered in silence until my husband and I were alone. After that, I started becoming increasingly needy and clingy in his view. I wanted to spend more time together to make up for the feelings of loss, but this was too much for him. He decided to leave; he wanted a divorce. Upon returning from a European trip, I found boxes with his personal items packed. He was very generous to me, leaving material things behind for me, but my heart was broken. My parents loaded me into their car and sped off to San Antonio. I was a basket case.

Death and Divorce: two mountains in the middle of my journey of life that I had not expected. *'How will I deal with these?'* I asked myself as the mountains loomed before me. It was only through much soul searching and crying out to the Lord that I surrendered to His plans for my life. I found out that He is a good God and did not cause the bad things. But how could this be? I learned that there is truly a curse on this earth and that the enemy of our soul is here to steal, kill, and destroy.

The next "mountain" appeared about four years later. It was after my divorce during a spiritual awakening when I began to devour the Word of God and learn about healing. Little did I know that this was to prepare me for that next mountain: the "mountain" of Disease. I had been dating a great Christian guy who went to my church and one night, after he left my house, my world began spinning out of control. I had changed into a silky wrap bathrobe and was checking to make certain that I had locked the back door. As my hand breezed across my chest, tying the wrap, I felt a hard, large knot in my right breast. *'I will call my breast doctor in the morning,'* I thought. He had been watching a lump in that same breast since I was about thirteen years old. I was thirty-three.

I called the doctor's office the next morning and was later notified to get a mammogram so they could compare it with a previous one. I recall looking up at the vents of the window unit in front of me as I held the land line phone and waited nervously for the results. The findings were that I had dense breast tissue with calcifications. Somehow, that did not give me relief.

The doctor called me into his office where he performed a needle biopsy. When he inserted it, no fluid was found, which was indicative of a cyst. No fluid was not a good indication, which I did not find out until much later. Cell phones were not in existence as we know today so our information base was very limited. The doctor said he would "watch it".

It was during a regular visit with my gynecologist that he insisted I go see the breast doctor that day. During the breast exam, the breast doctor observed the lump rising out of my breast. He suggested that I make an appointment with a plastic surgeon.

As I looked back on this at a later date, it appeared as if he was more interested in saving my breast than saving my life! The lump was larger than a golf ball and my right arm sometimes ached.

I never made the appointment with the plastic surgeon. Instead, my boyfriend insisted that I go to see his friend, another local surgeon. After examining me, he said I was a candidate for a double mastectomy, confirming that I had fibrocystic breast disease. My mama suggested I see a Houston surgeon, so I called my Houston gynecologist who referred me to Dr. Peter Fisher. I indeed agreed with the verse in Proverbs: "....in the abundance of counselors there is safety."

Off to Houston I traveled with Mama to an appointment with Dr. Fisher. At one point he performed another biopsy in his office, taking samples and sending them off to a lab. We later returned to his office to get the satisfying results: no cancer found. That was in April, but Dr. Fisher suggested removal of the lump when school was out, just to make certain.

I was a teacher; I completed my school duties early in May and scheduled my hospital visit later that same month. I felt I needed to have all of this behind me as I was scheduled to teach dance at Art Camp that summer, or so I thought.

I remember Mama driving me to Houston once again, this time for the removal of the lump. Faith-filled, she said to me, "Everything is going to be fine, no cancer." I agreed with her verbally, but in my heart, I felt a contradiction. The Holy Spirit does warn us of things to come.

I was put to sleep in a facility across the street from Houston Methodist Hospital. When I was barely awake from the anesthesia, Dr. Fisher was hovering over me telling me that it was cancer and that he was sending me across the street to the hospital to perform scans to ensure that cancer had not spread to my bones, brain, or liver. How could it be cancer when the tissue sample hadn't shown anything? I found out that I was one of ten women in America at the time who had a cancer growing around, over, and through an innocent, benign lump. A very unusual phenomenon, so much so that a student under Dr. Fisher wrote a paper about me.

I was alone as I lay on the bed, being transported for the scans. I saw no one except for the attendant and the hospital techs. I quietly prayed for good reports and knew that my mother was praying for me. It was God's grace that kept me calm. Our prayers were answered, as there was no cancer in any of the areas Dr. Fisher had mentioned, but the battle had just begun.

Dr. Fisher admitted me to the hospital, and we waited for surgery the next week. Back then, around thirty-seven years ago, insurance covered much longer hospital stays. I was to have a modified radical mastectomy, which meant removal of my right breast and some lymph glands. During this time, I notified my church; they immediately began praying for me. I began asking God if I was to have this surgery to please confirm it. He did with a calm peace and so I waited for my surgery date, though I also found anger arising. I was so angry at the enemy of my soul for this attack on my body that I decided on an interesting counterattack: praying for other patients in rooms down the hall. Clothed in my blue hospital gown, I would knock on their doors and ask if I could pray with them. Mama sometimes joined me in this battle. No one refused the invitation to prayer. I remember one woman having anxiety regarding surgery and another was concerned about her insurance approval. It was a very exciting adventure, doing the work of the Lord!

Finally, the day of my surgery arrived, and God showed Himself strong on my behalf. I was watching a TV preacher early that morning and he quoted a scripture about God never leaving or forsaking us. Then when I was wheeled downstairs by a nurse to the hospital chapel, the chaplain who led the service used the same scripture emphasizing that God would never leave or forsake us! That was confirmation, a message from God to me, one that He wanted me to hear.

Hebrews 13:5, "...I will never leave or forsake you..."

So on that day, as I went into surgery, I went forth with peace knowing that the God of this universe was with me and would not leave me alone. I awoke from the surgery with my right breast gone, but feeling little pain, as the nerves in my chest had been cut. What a blessing! Back in the room my father and brother arrived, telling me jokes and causing me to place a pillow over my stomach and chest because I was laughing so hard. Then my boyfriend, George, who soon afterward became my fiancé, arrived and of course all things were better. Yes, he asked a woman who had only one breast to marry him.

Before I left the hospital, I was informed that I had several lymph nodes involved, meaning that they had cancer in them, so I would need chemo and radiation. It was agreed upon that I would have the treatment in my hometown. When I was released from the hospital, I stayed with a very best friend in Houston for several days. George drove me home, where I did arm stretches walking my fingers up the wall so I could get my mobility back on my right side.

 I wish I could tell you that chemo was a breeze and that all was well, but the truth is that it was a very challenging time for me - the most difficult part of the journey. I was told that I would not lose all of my hair, but when I saw pieces of it on the shower floor, I began to cry. I was also told that the chemo would probably make me sterile. George had proposed to me so when I told him this, he said we would just adopt, no problem. I knew he loved children, so this broke my heart. Yet I was not willing to accept the prognosis. I kept praying the Scriptures and believing the opposite of what I was told would happen. I prayed over my oral chemo, Zechariah 4:7, that the chemo would only kill the bad cells but would not harm the good. Then when I began intravenous chemo, I once again prayed over the medicine. The nurse would wheel the chemo machine filled with medicine into the room, leave it there, and walk out of the room to return later. I would pray after she left, confessing no side effects. And every time there were none!

 After months of this, I ran into church one day and told a friend who was believing with me, "I'm still having my period!" Who gets excited about their monthly flow? I did! That meant I wasn't sterile!

 The fall and winter months of chemo were pretty much times of isolation, except for George and his cousin's wife, Cheryl, who was an angel who came and did crafts with me. It seemed like people avoided me, as if they thought cancer was contagious. I am sure it was only because they did not know what to say or how to act but this caused me to be very lonely. It was the only time that I got frustrated and asked God why this was happening to me? He never answered. It was during this time that I searched my heart, making sure I had forgiven everyone, especially my ex-husband. There is a link between unforgiveness and disease, as well as forgiveness and healing.

I read of King Hezekiah in 2 Kings 20:1-4, who was supposed to die but pled with the Lord, and God then said He would heal him. I did the same. I also attended church and was prayed for at the altar, having the pastor "lay hands on me" which is Biblical. I read my Bible and many scriptures leapt off of the page. Words like rhema - Holy Spirit words to me in the moment - such as Isaiah 43:2 "When you pass through the waters, I will be with you and through the rivers, they will not overwhelm you. When you walk through the fire, you will not be scorched, nor will the flame burn you." I also read of the accounts of Jesus healing the sick. These were like personal love letters with promises to me.

At the end of chemo, I did not take radiation. I felt totally drained and weakened by the chemo. I had read that you can over medicate and then your body can't fight back. I prayed about it and asked God to move on my oncologist since I never got an answer about whether to proceed or not. One day he came into the room and said, "Let's don't do it!" I totally agreed. Instead, I got married a month after chemo ended, fuzzy hair from sparse hair, and all! My husband has always said it did not matter to him if I had only one breast. I knew he really loved me, not just my body.

I got pregnant a couple of years afterwards despite the oncologist warning me that my eggs could be damaged from the chemo. Our miracle boy was conceived, which was actually a double miracle because I was on bed rest most of the pregnancy due to my incompetent cervix, even with it sewed shut! He is now grown, married, and growing his own family.

My life has had many bumps, many mountains in the road and I still have a few to overcome. I am not special, nor do I think of myself as such. I am just here to tell of the goodness of God. What He did for me, He can do for you. I repeat, He is no respecter of persons. We only need to believe that He will, not that He might. Too often we look at other people's experiences around us and don't believe God's word. We must not! Healing scriptures kept me alive and still do. Nehemiah 1:10 says, "Affliction shall not rise up a second time." You may not have the same "mountains" but know that God is the mountain mover! There is a curse on the earth that began in the Garden of Eden when man gave authority of this earth over to Satan. This caused a chasm between God and man, but God sent His only Son, Jesus, to the earth to be the sacrificial lamb and to bridge the chasm between God and man. If you haven't accepted Jesus as your Lord and Savior, you can do so today. Believe in your heart and go tell someone what you did. Then find a church preaching the uncompromised word of God. Watch God move in your behalf.

Often I think about Jesus, the lover of my soul. I get "tickled" and laugh out loud. I've always thought it was just the supernatural joy of the Lord but now I know that He has me laughing at the future because no matter what mountain looms before me, God can flatten it, for He is good!

Contact Information:
Denise LeDoux Leiato
Worship Leader
www.facebook.com/denise.leiato

Faithful Then, Faithful Now

DeAnna D. Cavenah

As I stood in that cold emergency room watching the nurse insert a needle that looked at least six inches long into my husband's leg, I knew something was desperately wrong when he asked her to let him know when she was going to do it. As she turned to look at me, I'll never forget the look on her face and the nauseating feeling in the pit of my stomach.

It seemed like any other normal Friday workday for me. I worked a nine to five job at a Pipe and Supply company in a nearby city five days a week while my husband worked as a scaffold builder at a local plant four days a week, off on Fridays. We were a young couple in our first year of marriage with a brand-new baby boy. I had decided to not work after our baby was born but then couldn't pass up the offer for a raise when my boss presented it. A raise was a great incentive for me and the only way I could return since I would need to hire a babysitter.

I really enjoyed my job, but on that particular Friday afternoon, February 22,1991, something felt very off. It was around four o'clock, just one hour before I was to clock out and I had such an uneasy feeling come over me. My first thought was, '*I need to leave, I do not feel good.*' Then my second thought was, '*This is crazy, you have one more hour left, toughen up.*' So that's what I did. My mother-in-law was taking care of Michael, our baby boy, that day so I knew before I could drive straight home, I would need to go pick him up. On the drive there, for some unknown reason, I decided to take a different route than I would normally take. It did not seem too odd at the time, but little did I know the reason would unfold within the next hour.

When I arrived at my in-law's home, they were watching Michael in the back room on the bed; he had just begun to really laugh and make all those irresistibly cute baby sounds. I can still remember so vividly that little all-in-one yellow outfit he had on as he giggled and cooed. Babies seem to know exactly how to bring a smile to your face and fill a room with joy. It seemed to go on for only a few short minutes before joy quickly faded into the background as my sister-in-law frantically rushed into the room telling my mother-in-law she needed to speak to her in the other room. I could not make out everything she was telling her, but I knew it was something bad. She did not want me to know, because when she came into the room, she said, "I can't tell you in front of DeAnna." I thought, *'This is ridiculous. I'm going in there.'* They stopped talking when I came around the corner and just looked at me. My sister-in-law was a crying mess, and my mother-in-law looked shocked and full of disbelief at what she had just been told.

As I looked at my sister-in-law she said, "I don't want to tell you."

I demanded she tell me what was wrong. She then proceeded with the news.

It was probably around 5:45 in the afternoon at that point. Earlier that day, possibly around 4:30 PM, my husband, Greg, and his oldest brother, Pete, along with one of their cousins had gone down to family property to cut some trees to help him build a porch. As Greg proceeded to cut one of the trees the chainsaw became wedged in the tree, and it would not budge. It was a very windy day and probably not the best of conditions to begin a project of this nature. Regardless, the guys were on a mission, and they were going to get the job done. Greg knew there wasn't much he could do at that point and decided to walk away and take a break. As he began to walk away the wind began to pick up speed and the trees began to sway as if they were dancing in rhythm. Pete noticed the tree they were attempting to cut down had been cut into just enough for it to begin to topple. As he realized what was happening, and the tree was about to fall, he shouted, "GREG THE TREE IS FALLING, RUN!" Without looking behind him and without hesitation, that's exactly what he did. Little did he realize the tree was falling in his direction. The tree was falling at a greater speed than he was capable of out-running. The very tall, healthy pine hit him in the back throwing his body several feet.

Earlier I wrote that I had an uneasy feeling at work and that I had taken a different route to my in-law's home that day. I truly believe that this was the reason for both. Before you marry your soon-to-be spouse, you are two individual people, but when you join in the union of marriage the Bible teaches that the two become one. I truly feel my spirit was engaged letting me know that my husband was in danger. I was still young and immature in my walk with the Lord at the time and did not realize that what was happening to me was a spirit of intercession for my husband. The Holy Spirit will warn us when things aren't right and prompt us to pray. Had I taken the normal route that day I would have driven up on the scene of the accident. I'm not quite sure how I would have handled that, but God obviously knew and spared me from seeing the devastation.

After sharing the news, my sister-in-law and I immediately jumped into her little yellow sportscar to head to the hospital where the ambulance was transporting Greg. My Father-in-law stayed behind waiting for my mother to come pick up the baby.

That was probably the wildest and scariest ride I had ever been on. As my sister-in-law drove at a high rate of speed with her flashers on, it seemed to me the other people on the road were driving without a brain. I know that may sound ugly, but I was taught when someone is driving with flashers on there is obviously an emergency, and I need to get into the other lane or pull off the road altogether. Needless to say, I had much road rage that evening.

When we finally arrived at the hospital I had one thing on my mind: "Get me to my husband now." As I stood in that cold emergency room watching the nurse insert a needle that looked at least six inches long into my husband's leg, I knew something was desperately wrong when he asked her to let him know when she was going to do it.

God is so very strategic in our everyday life. His Word says that the steps of a righteous man (or woman) are ordered of the Lord according to Psalm 37:23. The nurse that was on duty that day was a Christian lady that I had known all of my life and was a dear friend of our family. She was such a comfort to me that day. She looked at me with such compassion in her eyes and then looked at him and said, "Greg, I've already done the procedure." From that moment I realized that our life as we knew it had taken a drastic change.

There I stood in a hospital emergency room as a young married twenty-one-year-old woman with a four-month-old baby and the news I received was that my young, strong, handsome, new husband was now paralyzed. Wow! Life sure does know how to throw us some curve balls.

I had so many thoughts and questions going through my mind, but at the same time, I was thanking God for my husband's life. In all reality, I could have been standing there as a young twenty-one-year-old widow, but the Lord spared his life and because of that, I knew there had to be a purpose behind what we were facing.

The results from the x-rays and all the tests showed that Greg had sustained injuries resulting in T6 and T7 breaks and tearing of the spinal cord which left him paralyzed from the waist down. After a few days of treatment and being in the intensive care unit, the doctor took us into the family conference room. He told us that at that point Greg should have gotten feeling back into his lower extremities, and because he had not, they were diagnosing him as paraplegic, and he would live like that for the rest of his life. This was not a diagnosis I was expecting or willing to receive. The next two weeks I lived at the hospital, many nights in the waiting room cuddled up in a chair covered with a blanket until Greg was moved to a regular room.

Our next steps were to get him into a rehabilitation hospital. In an instant, we went from a two-income household to a no-income household. I felt the weight of the world on my shoulders. I am forever grateful that I was raised in a Christian home that taught me that God still performs miracles and that anything is possible to the person who puts their faith and trust in Him. It was at this point in my life I leaned upon the Lord like no other previous time and began my journaling journey. I truly believe I received my Life Verse at that time, although I truly didn't realize it until many years later, "I can do *all* things through Christ who gives me strength" Philippians 4:13. The Lord really did infuse me with a strength and a faith I didn't realize I had. There was so much that had to be dealt with physically and financially, not to mention emotionally.

The hospital where we were was not capable of handling a spinal cord injury, so we needed to find a place for treatment. In order to be moved to a rehabilitation hospital, we first had to be approved for Medicaid, which I was told could take quite some time. In spite of what I was told, we were approved within a couple of days. This approval covered 100% of the care that my husband was going to need. This was only the beginning of many other miracles that followed. I remember standing in the bathroom at the hospital talking with a dear sweet lady from our church, Ms. Reda DeMary, asking her if I was in faith or denial because I saw my husband walking and not paralyzed. She encouraged me that I was operating in faith. So I used that same faith in every situation and decision that I was making. Neither my husband nor myself could work during that time, so that meant no money. We had a small apartment, we had vehicles, we had doctors and hospital bills from our son being born, I had a student loan, and the list of expenses went on. I found myself as one of those people I had only heard stories about, having to live by faith and trust God for every need.

As one example, my mom and I met with our City Mayor of Kinder at the time, Fred Ashey. I remember sitting across the desk from him, telling him of our situation and that I was there to apply for a HUD (government assistance) apartment. He said, "You're asking for a miracle because there are people that have been on this list for months and some even years."

I said, "It's okay. I believe in miracles." I believe it was about two weeks and we were approved for a HUD apartment in the same apartment complex we lived then. We were also relieved from every one of our outstanding debts. My GYN and the hospital where I gave birth canceled our debt. My student loan was eradicated. Tell me God can't do it! He was moving mountains for us.

The day finally came when we were going to be transported to the Rehabilitation Hospital of Baton Rouge, Louisiana, which was two hours away from where we lived. The old life we once knew was no more and our new life had begun. I can look back now and say, "It was only by the grace of God." I'm not sure how we would have gotten through that time of our life without Him. God had gone before us and prepared everything that we would need for our new journey.

When we arrived at the facility it was quite an adjustment. We met staff, doctors, and patients. We learned quickly that most of them did not believe in miracles, and it was evident by the way they talked. Most were negative and didn't give us much hope. Basically, they were going to do their job, which was to train Greg to learn how to do life from a wheelchair and train me how to care for him. In the beginning of this transition, Greg had come to the realization that he was unable to provide and care for his new little family, much less for himself. Although he was discouraged, he was also a man of faith and had been raised in a Christian home and was taught the same things I had learned. This was a great opportunity for him to tap into that, and as he did, it became his very lifeline. During the day he would go through much therapy and when he wasn't in therapy, he was in the Word of God. Visiting hours didn't start until the evening so I wasn't allowed to stay with him during the day. Although I was not allowed to stay with him, the Lord had me in some therapy of my own during the day.

Our transition to Baton Rouge had both of us living under different circumstances. Because of the uncertainty from day-to-day activities and such a stressful transition, we thought it best that our baby live with our parents from week to week. They agreed to drive to Baton Rouge every weekend and bring him so we could spend time with him. There were so many "firsts" I missed as a new mom. I missed finding Michael's first tooth; I missed him standing on his own and taking his first steps. Wow, looking back, again, all I can say is that it was by the grace of God we came through.

The first few weeks, I lived with my sister's best friend and her family. I slept on their living room pull-out couch. I am forever grateful for their compassion and generosity during the difficult move. The Lord soon opened a door for me to go live with my church choir director's mom and dad, who were retired Presbyterian Pastors, for the next four months. They gave me my own room, which just so happened to be their "Faith Library." I don't believe there are any accidents in the Kingdom of God. He is very strategic in our lives. I also had my own key, so I was able to come and go without interrupting their lives. Their daughter, my very good friend and choir director at the time, Rena Beadle, also came to live there for a short while as she gave birth to her second son, David, while her husband was in another city working.

On the weekends they would go to the Rehabilitation Hospital where Greg was staying and pick him up and we would all go to church together. It was very important to us to find a church that we could call home and get support from while we were unable to attend our church back home. We also remained faithful to give back to the Lord what was His. We would always tithe on any offering or money that came into our life. We've always lived by the principle, "If it's not enough to meet my need, it must be a seed."

During the day while Greg was digging into the Word and taping scriptures all over the walls of his room, I was reading or driving around Baton Rouge singing and praising my way through this storm. Praise and Worship was my weapon of choice. Worship is one of the greatest weapons to defeat the enemy, build our faith, and strengthen us in any and every season. The Rehab sent the psychiatrist in to see Greg because they thought he was depressed and that he wasn't facing the reality he would never walk again. He told them, "This is my reality, the Word of God, and I will walk again."

Greg became an inspiration to all he came in contact with during his stay in the Rehabilitation Facility. He had a great attitude, and patients would often visit his room. I remember one elderly man, Mr. Geyban, who absolutely loved Greg. He was an ornery gentleman who wouldn't allow anyone to feed him, but he befriended Greg and would ask for him to come and feed him crackers. Greg developed such a compassionate heart not only for the patients but for the staff as well.

On April 26, 1991, Greg started to get a little movement in his left leg. Of course, nurses tried to tell him it was only spasms, but we knew differently and when they realized it wasn't just spasms, they started more intense therapy. God was doing exactly what He said He would do: raise Greg up to walk again!

On May 6, 1991, Greg walked for the first time with assistance. The therapy once again increased. On May 25th, he walked with a walker, and once again therapy was increased. We continued to see progress. He was a living testimony to all of the patients and their families, and it gave them much hope. He told them, "I'm walking out of this place." That's exactly what he did on September 7, 1991. He walked out! He was such an inspiration and testimony in that place that he was featured in the Baton Rouge Newspaper.

It was quite an adjustment the many months after his return home. Although he was no longer paralyzed, he still walked with a cane and could not return to the job he once had. Our roles had reversed quite a bit: I was the one who worked a full-time job outside of the home. During the months and years that would follow, we saw God's hand continue to move in miraculous ways for us. Greg's body not only became stronger, but our finances increased as a job opened up for him to work for the United Postal Service.

John 10:10 (AMP) says, "The thief (satan) comes only in order to steal and kill and destroy. I came that they may have life, and have it in abundance (to the full, till it overflows)."

The enemy feared our future, so he tried to destroy our lives both physically and emotionally. God does not cause chaos, confusion, or bad things such as the accident, but He definitely works in the midst of it all.

Romans 8:28 (AMP): "And we know (with great confidence) that God (who is deeply concerned about us) causes *all* things to work together (as a plan) for good for those who love God, to those who are called according to His plan and purpose." *Emphasis added.*

I don't have all the answers concerning why we had to go through everything we did, especially at such a young age, but I do know that God's timing and ways are perfect. He already had the blueprint for our lives mapped out, saw into our future, and knew exactly where we would be today.

Isaiah 55:8-9 (NKJV): "For My thoughts are not your thoughts, nor are your ways My ways," says the Lord. "For as the heavens are higher than the earth, so are My ways higher than your ways, and My thoughts than your thoughts."

God's plan for our lives far exceeded anything that we could have planned for ourselves and our family, which, by the way, has increased to two sons and a granddaughter. His plan went beyond just us. It involved His heart, and His heart is people. I truly believe that we both started our on-the-job training while living in Baton Rouge.

After moving home and adjusting to the changes, we became deeply involved in many areas of ministry within our local church body and also outside of the church. Greg ministered for seventeen years weekly at both the prison and the Allen Parish Mental Health Facility where he later became Chaplain.

God is still proving Himself Faithful to us. He was Faithful then and He is Faithful now. Greg is still employed with the United States Postal Service, and I am overwhelmingly grateful and thankful to say that we have been serving as full-time pastors for seventeen years of a thriving church called Full Life Assembly located in Louisiana. The church name says it all; we are living the "Full Life" and doing so with such amazing and beautiful people.

I can confidently say and stand on this scripture, "I am clothed with strength and dignity, and I laugh without fear of the future." Proverbs 31:25 (NLT)

I know that whatever comes my way, God is well able to take care of me and my family. He took two people that were the most unlikely to succeed, that had a very unfortunate accident, and turned them into a miracle and testimony that would affect generations to come. It's a testimony that keeps on giving hope to the hopeless and encouragement to the weak. He is not only our Protector but our Provider, our total source of supply.

"The Lord is my light and my salvation; Whom shall I fear? The Lord is the strength of my life; Of whom shall I be afraid?" Psalm 27:1 (NKJV)

Contact Information:
DeAnna Cavenah
Author. Speaker. Worship Pastor.
www.dequincyfulllife.com

She Laughs Without Fear of Her Season

Booth #5 - Vintage and Grace

Victoria Bennett

I want to begin by saying I'm proud of you. It takes faith to be where you are. I'm sharing some of my experiences with you, in hopes that no matter where you find yourself, you'll be filled with hope, able to pick yourself up and reclaim your life and joy. There will be a seed planted in your soul that will grow and sustain you in the days ahead. I believe you'll be refreshed and will have seen Jesus. If you're still breathing, you still have purpose and hope. This too, shall pass. Know that if He can do it for me, He can do it for you, sister!

Backtrack with me to 2022. I had two cervical spine surgeries, resulting in two rods, a cage, and twelve screws in my neck! The recovery and new way of life from that has been quite a journey. There's a new level of trust gained, essential to my mental health and everyone else's around me. The most recent developments show there's a bone spur in my middle back and arthritis in my lower back. I didn't receive this report, however, and I chose to stand for the healing Jesus died for until I see a miracle! I wouldn't wish this pain on my worst enemy. With great pain comes great growth. It's not always easy because we fight our flesh and the enemy of our souls, Satan. But with Jesus Christ, we can do *all* things, according to Philippians 4:13.

Fast forward to 2024. I found myself facing a set of crossroads as the job I felt was my answered prayer to a lifelong career abruptly came to a halt.

Leaving work, crying out in physical pain, I felt like a failure. My soul was screaming! I was holding a boulder in my stomach as I pondered on what just happened and the results to follow. I was thriving and loving my career as a Biller\Collector. I was blessed with Christian leadership and people who fought to stay up, no matter what. Thick and thin. I felt as if I'd have given up on my work family. *'How did I get here? How is it the place I came to call my work home, is now just a memory? How did I allow myself to continue working in such pain? Am I ever going to get better? How will my husband and I make it financially now?'* Those hopeless questions were quickly becoming a rabbit hole with no end.

The pain started increasing rapidly and was so severe I was completely debilitated. The board which I was confident would be there for my next step, was ripped out from under me. I was facing the unknown for what was next in my life. Each crossroad in life for me pretty much comes down to two paths, life or death. Life in this moment meant quitting my career to rest and heal. Death meant continuing my career and facing debilitating pain. Physically I couldn't take it anymore and was forced to pick life. Life felt like death in so many ways.

I've come to believe life will always bring us to crossroads and trials to keep us on our knees. We then reach out to whatever we believe will fill the void and bring peace as quickly as possible. As humans, we tend to reach for instant relief that is tangible or familiar. I call these "empty fillers". Substitute void fillers often leave us emptier and lead to more pain. I almost always used to reach for "empty fillers". The truth is, the only "thing" that can fill a void, is the creator of the creation containing the void. Coming to know my Creator, meant coming to know the One who would become my void filler. He has begun a transformative work in me and my life. It is all part of a greater and necessary process. I wish I could say I don't ever grab for "empty fillers" anymore, but that would be a lie. I can however attest to the faithfulness of God to take those voids and satisfy them, preventing me from having to reach for anything else. It's here in the tasting and seeing that the Lord is so good that I discovered the ability to laugh at whatever the future brings.

After several weeks, the pain began to slow. I hadn't gone without pain in a very long time. Excitement flowed through me! I began making plans, started to do household chores and got active again. I saw a light in this dark place of pain in which I had become a long-term resident. I felt I had rested and was going to return to work. I quickly learned this wasn't the case as the pain returned. I had to put my big girl pants on. I was in a fight for my life, and I didn't know whether I'd lay down and quit or keep fighting forward in faith. If I quit, my entire life would've been in vain. If I fought, I knew I would have hope and would see victory. The answer seemed so obvious, but I was tired, and my flesh was weak. Being in a fight with chronic pain that seems never-ending will wear a person down!

I heard of a new flea market in town, and I decided to rent a booth. To my surprise, my booth number was five! I was excited. Five is the number for grace and favor. Now I needed a name. After much contemplation, "Vintage and Grace" was my choice. I loved it! It just had a ring to it. I began filling it with many treasures, both old and new. I began getting lost in this booth, constantly looking for what I could add. This became my "empty filler". What I really needed was physical rest and rest in Christ.

Rest isn't a word that I'm familiar with. I've always related it to laziness and unworthiness. I was raised by my great grandmother and there were always things to be done. I wasn't rewarded for resting. I was rewarded for working hard. Through college and work, rest wasn't rewarded. The harder I pushed and the more I achieved, the more I was rewarded. I'm a hard worker, and this has always been an escape amid the trials of my life. I know how to busy myself and I've been blessed with "smarts" and the ability to do things well. Booth #5 became my next achievement to avoid dealing with the issues at hand. I knew better, but I still grabbed for the quick relief and what was familiar.

In some quiet time with the Lord, I asked "What am I supposed to learn in this season?"

 He said, "A new level of trust."

With an attitude, I said, "How many levels of trust is there in this thing?"

If this sounds unfamiliar with the way God deals with you, remember every child is unique and He deals with us individually, in ways we can understand. We have very honest and sometimes tough, dialogues. I've learned I can trust my Father and He wants to hear the truth of my emotions, so He can help me with them. He wants the same from you. He loves you so much and wants to be "I AM" to you. He can be anything and provide anything we need. He's the God of the impossible and I can testify to that firsthand. I've seen God use my trials to grow and mature me, while bringing me closer to Him.

One of my favorite pieces of furniture is my vintage vanity from my great grandma. It's old, but beautiful, and still very useful. It reminds me of her and brings a sense of peace when I put on makeup and fix my hair in front of it. Vintage implies something is of high quality and from the past. Let me tell you what! I have some stories to tell that are vintage. Lessons learned that carry over to the next seasons in life and are of high quality. Remembering the testimony of God's faithfulness through trials of the past brings so much strength to me now.

Grace is the free, undeserved favor of God we see through salvation and blessings. Grace is what is given to others when they deserve punishment, but forgiveness is shown instead. Grace can be given to ourselves when we need to accept that we're human and make mistakes. Being hard on others or ourselves is our natural response, but grace takes effort and love. If it wasn't for grace, I don't know where I'd be! Learning to give and accept grace became a key component to my survival in that season. This is an art! I'm just sayin'.

Looking back over God's goodness and faithfulness in my life, there were times where I made it through and had no clue how. Hindsight revealed it was only by staying anchored in the promises of my Father - the only One who will never let me down. It revealed how the Lord orchestrated a beautiful symphony that produced a redemptive work in me. Deuteronomy 31:6 ESV says, "Be strong and courageous. Don't fear or be in dread of them, for it's the Lord your God who goes with you. He will not leave you or forsake you." I had to remind myself I don't have to fear. I can choose to trust Him and be strong. If He led me before, He will lead me again. If He provided before, He will provide again. If He made a way in the impossible situations, He will make a way again.

Going back to my childhood, I was raised Catholic and never had a real encounter with the love of God that I could honestly remember. I attended a Holy Spirit filled church service with my mom and brother at the age of sixteen, and there I had an encounter that redirected my life. I went to the front for an alter call. The pastor laid hands on me and down I went! I was slain in the Holy Spirit and knew nothing about that. I was used to a church where if you coughed loud, you were out of line. I started rolling and laughing once I hit the ground. A holy roller, in all my glory. I was on the floor for thirty minutes! I had no cares in the world. Once I was able to regain my natural conscience, I stood up, covered in sweat and looking around like a deer in headlights. I walked back to my seat, unsure of what had taken place. I felt different. I felt everything I was facing would be okay because God loved me and knew me. I left that service and threw out CD's, cigarettes, weed, and wept in repentance the entire drive home. From that day forward, I had a newfound confidence in Christ, who gave it all so that I could have it all. He took on my sin, so we could live forever together. I wish I could say that my life was just dandy after that, but I can't. My life was tumultuous and lots of lessons would come through learning things the hard way.

My life as a sixteen-year-old wasn't typical, being raised by a great-grandmother who was raised during the Great Depression. There are a host of lessons and trials associated with this, but through it all, I grew. I was strengthened. I was extremely promiscuous and was the classic "looking for love in all the wrong places" case. I thought if a guy wanted me sexually, then I was worth loving. I did a lot of searching, to put it lightly! I was in more situations than most will ever experience, and God led me out in victory. I'm now married to a man that God sent me. I vowed my body back to God and showed the enemy that he no longer had control over me in that area. We did have a few slip ups while abstaining before marriage, but we took communion, repented and moved forward in grace. God strengthened me and rewarded me with an amazing husband. He took this disgrace and shame I felt and presented me holy and righteous. That's only possible with God!

Shortly after my encounter with God, my dad passed. I was blessed to have known he did love me. He was just broken and did the best he could. I knew he had a huge heart and was just hurting in this life. Losing my dad was supposed to be hard, but my emotions didn't respond that way. My memories from birth until five years old weren't the greatest. There was abuse and neglect due to his addiction. I do have a few happy memories I hold on to. He loved to laugh and smile; my relationship with him was prohibited once I moved in with my great grandmother at five years old. It was a constant battle between him and "Maw Maw" the times I did see him. When I turned thirteen, I told Maw Maw I wanted a relationship with him. She allowed me to go visit him. Those memories from thirteen to sixteen were mixed with love and pain, but I'm grateful for those years.

I graduated high school and enrolled at Louisiana State University at the age of eighteen. I moved out and got a place by school. I started a new job serving tables at Chili's and hit the books – both full-time. I had worked since I was thirteen, but this was a different level of responsibility. My mom moved in with me there. From that time on, the roles were reversed, and I operated more as the mother and she as the daughter. I was entangled in a codependent relationship with my mom. Till this day, we are relearning our roles as mother-daughter the correct way. Praise God she is sober now and taking on her new life and all God has called her to. Let's just say, it's been a very long road, but God has shown to be faithful! If He can change *my* mom, my friend, He can do *anything*!

Trying to balance all my responsibilities took all I had. Any free time, I was partying and taking anything that made me "feel" something other than stress and pain. Life has a way of pulling us back to the familiar "empty fillers". One night, I got the call that my brother was dying, and it didn't look like he'd make it. My mom was hysterical and said I needed to get there ASAP! He moved on to his permanent home that day, at only twenty-one years old. My brother was my world, my protector, and my rock. I was lost and didn't know how I'd make it. He was my best friend. I cannot express the pain I felt. I didn't understand. I asked God, "Why? Anything but this." I had one visit with a counselor and never went back. I continued moving forward, because that's what I do. That semester when finals came around, I wasn't motivated to study. I'd lost my drive. My brother had left a huge void, and I was empty. I didn't even want to finish school.

But God showed up! That one counsel session I completed? The counselor wrote a note on my behalf to my professors saying I needed extra time to take my finals. This was a light in my very dark valley. I thanked God over and over and drew closer to Him. My ability to trust God with my future was strengthened.

The day after I graduated LSU, my mom told me Maw Maw had terminal cancer. Pancreatic cancer is a killer, on a mission. I took this time to step away from my job and take care of Maw Maw with mom. I was able to give back some to her for taking care of me. Let's just say I'm not a natural when it comes to taking care of people. I was stretched in many ways! Love was the motivator when those tough moments would arise. I'd tell myself, "I can do anything for fifteen minutes," as I cleaned up her "messes". She passed away and I saw peace on her for the first time in a long time. I knew she went to her eternal home. Maw Maw had been the one to hold us all together, and now I had to take on this role for my mom and sister. I didn't know how I would make it through, but God held my hand and lead me. He taught me more trust in Him and proved His faithfulness.

I was twenty-one when Maw Maw passed. I struggled to keep my life together. I had become a daily drinker and smoker of marijuana to numb my bad feelings. I coasted through life in survival mode most of the time. I had to fake it to make it. Now, I faith it to make it! I always had the Holy Spirit inside of me, but I didn't tune in to hear Him a lot of the time. I was going down a road that really led nowhere good. The bad part was, it looked like I was doing pretty good on the outside. On the inside, I carried so much pain.

Several years passed on idle. At twenty-five, I ran into an old boyfriend at my stepbrother's wedding. He was my first serious boyfriend when I was thirteen. We had dated off and on for years, but it had been a few years since we had last connected. Looking back, he was never good for me. He had a great heart, but his brokenness had become a darkness in him that brought me much pain since the day we met. Out of the corner of my eye, I saw him walk by. We talked a bit and went about our day. The next day, he messaged me, and we decided to try this one last time. We moved in together and I was helping him raise his two girls. We moved to Lake Charles in 2017 after his house flooded in The Great Flood of 2016. We married in May that year.

Our relationship was very toxic. We both had so much pain and didn't know how to function together. I quit work and dedicated my life to my husband and the girls. The girls were such blessings to me and truly kept me grounded. They saw more than I'm proud of, but I believe God used this time of their lives to plant the seed of Jesus in their hearts that would bring forth good fruit. We had really great times and I knew he loved me. Then, we had really bad times and I felt completely broken, hopeless and lost. I was becoming someone I'm not, and we were having fewer good times. It wore me down, and looking back, he was getting tired too. We would fight, and I'd leave and then go back. It was a crazy cycle. I never knew what I'd do wrong next to get him mad. I'c lost touch with reality and my mind was fixated on keeping him happy. I just knew things would get better because we were in church, and we were trying. It just didn't seem to end. I gained fifty pounds in the marriage as I turned to food to fill the void.

During that time, we lost three babies. I really never wanted to get pregnant. My husband at that time was pretty forceful when he wanted something. My insurance lapsed and I was unable to have my birth control filled. He had all access to the money and wouldn't pay for it. He said, "You're going to have my baby!" Well, a few weeks later I was pregnant. At first, I was frustrated but when it set in that I had a baby inside of me, I got excited.

One afternoon I was feeling pretty badly. We went to the ER, and they sent me home saying I was fine. Later that night, I began feeling like I was dying, because I was! There was so much pressure; it felt as if my bottom was going to fall out. I had cold sweats and dizziness. After several grueling hours I told my husband we were going back to the hospital. They looked at me crazy initially, but once they reviewed the vaginal ultrasound, their attitudes changed. I had an ectopic pregnancy, still growing. I ruptured at nine weeks. I was hemorrhaging! They had me in surgery so fast, I don't remember much other than waking up. I lost my right fallopian tube and first child that day.

Shortly after, I was pregnant again. This time it was intrauterine. Around ten weeks, I miscarried. The doctor had me on pelvic rest for two weeks. My husband talked me into breaking that rest before it was time. Looking back, these are times I wish I would have stood up for myself; not just laid down and been taken advantage of over and over. However, this was how I'd become. A doormat.

I got pregnant a third time after all that trauma. This time I really struggled to be excited at all. I had been through so much at that point, and I really wanted out. I was a high-risk, so blood was drawn twice weekly. One morning my phone rang. The OBGYN instructed I get to the hospital because my bloodwork wasn't normal. That drive, in suspense only a few months prior, now was in dread and anger.

Guess what? Another ruptured, ectopic pregnancy. Immediate surgery was ordered *again* to remove the tube and baby. My feeling like a woman went out the window. I didn't feel worthy of anything. *'Was physical, sexual and mental abuse a factor in me not being able to sustain life in my womb? Was all this my fault? How'd I get here so fast? I can't have babies now? Really?'* I didn't understand, and I was mad at God. I still don't understand and have moments with tears. God has since shown me my babies went straight home, never to suffer. Not ever. The world is so insane today! It took total surrender to God in that empty place and hanging on to His faithfulness to pull through. Now I joke and laugh about my kids and how they'd get annoyed with me. I always joke why God didn't give me kids; because they would hate all my rules and living righteously speeches! I'm now blessed to have inherited three kids and three grandkids, with one on the way! Only God!

Fast forward to the latter months of our marriage. In March of 2020, I attended a Bible study: "I Do Boundaries". Finding the freedom to say "no" to my husband was the catalyst needed to bring change, and with boundaries up, I did notice a change. He moved in with another woman just as the quarantine for the global pandemic, COVID, began. I was left alone, and fear started a work. With flu-like symptoms and not eating or drinking, I passed out in my trailer and called someone using SIRI. I had the flu, but I swore I had COVID and wasn't going to make it. It felt like fear gripped me and I couldn't breathe. I learned how to tune in to the Holy Spirit like never before. I had messed my life up so badly; I knew the Lord had to lead every step to come. Even clinging to God, pulling out of this seemed impossible. Thankfully, we serve a God who specializes in impossible situations and bringing miracles from them.

My family, church family and friends were all key players in me finding freedom from that dark place. God provided in intimate ways. My fridge went out: someone blessed me with a new one. The TV's were all taken; God sent someone who replaced them all. The examples were never ending. My life started to look up. I had hope and freedom for the first time in what felt like a lifetime. God took care of everything I needed, plus some. Divorce is always hard and there is never an easy way to go through it. I saw the hand of God like never before in one of the toughest times of my life. This also caused me to rise up in prayer and faith, and I was strengthened as a woman of God. I learned my identity was in Christ alone. Nothing else. I learned boundaries and I got off the floor, retiring from being a doormat. If it wasn't for this marriage, I wouldn't have the church family I do and wouldn't be the woman I have become. I also wouldn't have the amazing husband I have now! God restored and redeemed my life after the darkest and most undeserving times.

To laugh at the future without knowing it requires trust in *who* holds the future. As children we sat back in the arms of someone who loved us, allowing them to hold us and plan our days because of blind trust. If I believe the Gospel through faith, then I can have that same childlike faith I had when I was first forgiven and redeemed. The One holding the planets and stars, that's Who holds your future. He is the master puzzle maker. He has each piece divinely ordained to be a certain shape and fit in a certain place at a certain time. We can only see one or two pieces, where He sees the entire picture, complete as a masterpiece.

Trials and crossroads are always going to come. The heat exposes what isn't healed and what's really in the heart. The Bible says trials are used to build our character to become like Christ. We must look inward and do a self-inventory of our faith. We must *choose* to walk by faith and not by sight. He knew we would only be able to muster enough faith to trust, that it would be as small as a seed. Then, God will take what you have, and from it grow more than you can ask, think, or imagine. Because of His love for us, He will accomplish the rest. We have the power to determine the course of our trials. We can have joy and hope or be discouraged and defeated. It's not easy but with the Holy Spirit we can do all things. He says, "Be still and know I am God." To be still, I must trust. To trust I must know Him. To know Him, I must spend time with Him in a relationship. Watching Him work in miraculous ways grows the trust and strengthens the relationship. But we *do* have a part to play. It is empowering to know we have the tools to overcome any trial we face! We're more than conquerors *in* Christ, who loves us, as Romans 8:37 says.

Thankfulness is key to pulling out of the dark times. It required me to dig deep but hope and truth returned. I would thank God for things I so often took for granted, such as my bed, breath, home, food, eyesight, walking, etc. Then, thankfulness started to overwhelm me. Surrounding myself with people that truly love me and spoke the truth was also vital. I needed to hear the hard things. Surrendering to God and blindly putting my faith in Him, expecting a move, was necessary.

When He shows up, because He always will, He then becomes all we need. He fights our battles. He vindicates us. He shows us the future. He strengthens us with joy and guides us through any trial with grace. It's often not how we think He should do these things either. His grace is enough for anything we face, our fault or not. His love will even use our mistakes for our good.

Nehemiah 8:10 says, "The joy of the Lord is our strength." Steal our joy. Steal our strength. Keep joy. Keep strength. My Maw Maw used to say, "I laugh to keep from crying!" I now understand this completely. Laughing meant I couldn't look at circumstances or the past or even the future. I must focus on Him. One service not long ago, I was filled with the joy of the Lord. I began laughing at the enemy. I couldn't stop laughing because I saw him in the spiritual realm, and it was so funny to me. The laughter increased as I saw his fiery darts. It is all based on lies. The enemy gets us distracted by using smoke and mirrors to deceive us. If we can look at the situation, and believe a lie, then we are already defeated. The humor was in the fact that he was so powerless. Once I composed myself, I was just in awe of how we live in fear and don't have to.

Vintage stories of God's love and grace make the crossroads I'm facing seem like nothing. I can laugh at what's to come because I know with no doubt, God will make a way. Resting in God, He'll lead the way. I'm not perfect, but I'm more mature than I used to be. I can face anything head on. I may not know what tomorrow holds, but I know Who holds it. I'll laugh and sing with joy because no matter what, He won't give up on me and I'm not giving up on Him. He has to come through, or it's all a lie! I wait in expectation of what He's doing next. His joy is my strength! You too my friend, can laugh at what's to come on this same strength - His joy.

Contact Information:
Victoria Bennett
Booth #5 – Vintage and Grace
facebook.com/groups/1103640528152733

Through the Storms

Zeni Pradel

In 2021 I was not laughing at the future and it took me until mid-2024 for me to really understand how I could and should be doing just that. During a period of one year, our family had three family members pass away. My heart felt like it was going to be forever broken, yet I still clung to just a little bit of hope that God was still in control somehow, even when I kept asking, "Why us?"

Everything started in 2021 when my Dad, Jose, was diagnosed with Lewy Body Dementia (LBD). Although I knew that one day my parents would no longer be with me, I was not prepared for my father to be so sick and for my mother to care for him all by herself, especially with them living five hours away from me.

My mother has always been a caregiver. She had not worked since she got married to my father, and she dedicated her life to taking care of her family. My parents were four days shy of reaching their 52nd anniversary when Dad gained his heavenly wings.

Throughout his complicated illness, he had to be Baker Acted three times due to his aggressiveness with my Mom, though obviously, this was no fault of his. Baker Acted is when someone has to be detained for mental health evaluation due to their illness for up to seventy-two hours. My Mom felt so guilty for having to do that, but her life was in danger during those times and she had no choice. She made it very clear when making the 911 call that he was a dementia patient. Thankfully, everyone involved (police and fire rescue) was very professional and understanding. Those calls were very frightening, but every single time, I made the five-hour drive from Miami to Ocala, no matter what time it was, so that I could be there for my parents through those difficult moments.

I made every effort to take trips to alleviate some of that burden from my mom. I went on weekends and requested to work from home for weeks at a time so that I could at least help out at night. I'm thankful that my husband was so supportive of me doing all this. In his words, "Your dad is our priority right now." My sisters were not able to be as present because they had their own children to care for and did not have the flexibility in their jobs as I did. I was thankful that I was able to help out our mom on behalf of *all* of us. I knew many families that didn't have even one person able to assist. We were very blessed.

My Dad passed away on October 13, 2022. I was sad but also relieved because I knew that he was with our Lord Jesus Christ and that he was no longer suffering. I was relieved because my mom didn't have to suffer seeing him deteriorate Still, there was sadness thinking that my mom was going to be alone five hours away from me. It was very hard to think that I couldn't do more for Mom at that moment. She didn't want to move to Miami, and I couldn't leave a job with the eligibility of retiring in three years with a full pension. We decided to ride it out and just see how God would lead us and how I could continue to support her emotionally, spiritually, and financially. I kept asking God to open doors that would allow me to do so much more for my family, but it just wasn't happening at the time.

On February 5, 2023, my father-in-law, Rene, passed away. He had suffered a couple of strokes and was never the same after that. One day I was at work and he was at his home. I decided to stop by to pay him a visit. He was already bedridden and giving up on life. I knew that he did not lead a life that was pleasing to the Lord, but I also knew that he loved the Lord and I wanted to make sure that he had a seat in heaven if he didn't get better. This was actually the first time that I had prayed the salvation prayer with someone. I remember when we finished, he looked at me and said, "I wish I would have done this a long time ago." That brought absolute tears of joy to my eyes. I knew at that point that he would be saved and he believed it too. It was hard seeing him suffering because he was scared of death; all I could do every time I saw him was to remind him of God's love, that it was okay to let go, and that God would be there waiting for him.

My husband and I both lost our fathers within a six-month period. There was a lot of sadness in our home. But we were grateful that our three children were there with us. We still had our mothers to care for and in the middle of it all, we just kept planning and dreaming of our future retirement to make sure that we were able to include our moms in it and be able to take care of them. Our kids are pretty much self-sufficient at this time (over twenty years old), and we knew that it would continue to be our turn to watch after our mothers.

What happened next was unimaginable. First, a little history. My daughter, Lizzie, and her fiance, Randy, had known each other for ten years, but they didn't start dating until three years after they met. I remember my daughter coming home after their first date and telling me how much she liked him. She even said that she felt he was the one! Imagine hearing that from your daughter at eighteen years old!

The day we met Randy, he came to our house. My middle daughter, Jessica was sixteen years old and somewhat shy. Randy took it upon himself to spend some time talking with her! He was getting to know her. They had so much in common! To us that meant the world because it was not just about Lizzie. This was all about getting to know Jessica and us a little at a time while dating Lizzie. No other guy had taken the time to really do that. We knew Randy would be very special.

Randy's and Lizzie's relationship grew very strong and they decided to move in together. One day, we were surprised with an ultrasound picture! We were so happy and couldn't wait for this new part of our life. On December 1, 2022, our granddaughter Amadi was born six weeks early due to Lizzie having pre-eclampsia. I don't think I need to say how hard this was on our family, but we all pulled through to make sure that they had everything they needed. Randy was able to stay home for two months with Lizzie and Amadi. Praise God for that because nothing would have prepared us for what happened nine months later.

On October 30, 2023, I had to get my ovaries taken out. I was home recovering that night when we received a call from Lizzie that Randy was not home yet. It was really late and it wasn't like him to not answer the phone or not call about being late. I was in a lot of pain from the surgery and I felt helpless. I told my husband, "We have to go to her. We need to be there." When we got there, the police were there letting my daughter know that Randy was in a car accident and was in critical condition. My husband took my daughter to the hospital and I stayed at her house with my son, Daniel, to watch after the baby. I wasn't going to be able to pick her up, but I had my son there to help me if need be. I prayed and prayed and prayed. I called our prayer line at church, I called my mom to do a prayer chain with her friends at church. I begged God to please get him through this. We all did.

A few hours later on October 31, 2023, Randy passed away leaving behind my daughter and their eleven-month-old child. Lizzie's life was forever changed at that moment. I knew then that we were going to have to step up 1000% to help her get through this and figure things out. It was very hard to think that she would now have to raise their baby girl by herself as a single mom. Yes, she had us and his family, but it was still a fact. Our lives forever changed that night and I couldn't understand. I asked all the why questions. Why did it have to happen to him? Why did God allow this to happen? Why didn't he save him from death? Why did he leave my daughter in so much pain? Why did he leave Amadi without her Papa? I'm not going to lie. I was very angry. Sad, but angry. I tried to keep things together for my daughter but the emotions were very hard to maneuver. It didn't matter how hard we tried to show Lizzie that we were there and that everything was going to be okay, she was *still* hurting and she would be for a very long time.

After a couple of weeks, Lizzie and Amadi moved in with us. This was another huge change for us, but our motto became "whatever it takes." Whatever it takes to help our daughter and granddaughter make it through, whatever it takes to make their lives as normal as possible, whatever it takes for them to know that they will be taken care of.

It took months of emotional rollercoasters on everyone's part but in the end, God showed us that everything would fal into place and that everyone would be ok. My daughter's relationship with us and with Jesus has been closer than it's ever been. Our retirement plans are uncertain, but I continue to trust God and the direction that he is taking my family and me in. I have seen the progress that our family is making through this difficult time. Some days we cry together and others we laugh together. But the moments that keep me laughing are the ones where we plan our vacations together, where we are able to take part in some of the milestones that our granddaughter is making, where we have deep conversations and can remember and laugh at past memories with our beloved Randy. There will always be a big hole in our hearts, but knowing that Randy is with our Lord Jesus Christ and will always be our angel is what keeps me laughing without fear of what the future holds for all of us, especially for my daughter and granddaughter.

The promises of God are real, my friend! If you are going through something very difficult, just know that God acknowledges we will have these challenges and hardships. He encourages us to have faith in his promises and to trust him during these difficult times. He promises to be with us, provide us with strength, and guide us through the storms of life. He will turn bad things into good things and He will forever love us.

Psalm 30:5
Weeping may stay for the night, but joy comes in the morning.

Jeremiah 29:11
For I know the plans I have for you," declares the Lord, "plans to prosper you and not to harm you, plans to give you hope and a future."

Romans 8:28 -29
And we know that in all things God works for the good of those who love him, who have been called according to his purpose.

Isaiah 43:1-2
"Do not fear, for I have redeemed you; I have summoned you by name; you are mine. When you pass through the waters, I will be with you; and when you pass through the rivers, they will not sweep over you. When you walk through the fire, you will not be burned; the flames will not set you ablaze."

Romans 15:13
May the God of hope fill you with all joy and peace as you trust in him, so that you may overflow with hope by the power of the Holy Spirit.

Hang on to his promises and you too will be okay.

Contact Information:

Zeni Pradel
Zeni Designed Company
https://zenidesignedco.etsy.com

Trusting God in Every Season

Lesa Dale

Proverbs 31:25 says, "She is clothed with strength and dignity; she can laugh at the days to come." This verse has always resonated deeply with me. It encapsulates the essence of a woman who trusts God so completely that she can face the future with joy and confidence. Reflecting on my life, I see countless instances of God's provision and guidance that have taught me to laugh at the future, knowing He holds it in His hands.

God has always inspired me to give, a calling I recognized early on as a spiritual gift. Over the years, this gift has led me to serve on the finance committee at church and spend thirteen years coordinating Financial Peace classes. I even trained as a financial coach through Dave Ramsey's program, helping others build secure financial foundations. But as I've grown, I've come to see that God's abundance goes far beyond financial provision alone.

Now, when I speak on God's abundance, my focus is not just on finances but on seeing His provision in every part of life. My journey has moved from financial provision to a more profound clarity about God's abundance. As I share my story, I hope you'll see that the same God who cared for me and my family over the years has an abundance of grace, love, and provision waiting for all of us.

The Antique Vanity and the Envelope System

In the corner of my room stands an antique wooden vanity, a cherished heirloom inherited from my great-aunt. Its polished, warm-toned wood gleams with a history of care, intricate carvings, and brass drawer pulls tell a story of days gone by. The centerpiece, a majestic round mirror slightly fogged with age, reflects countless memories of mornings spent in front of it.

I didn't use this vanity for beauty products or jewelry. Instead, it became the heart of my financial system. In front of the mirror sat three boxes: an antique jewel box, pink with hand-painted flowers; a wooden jewel box with exquisite carvings; and a plain glass box. Each box had a specific purpose—one for tithes, one for extra expenses like my boys' activities, and one for the bank deposit on Fridays.

As a single mom working as a waitress, I brought home cash daily and was paid in cash on Fridays. This system, guided by my faith, helped me manage my finances effectively. Every time I received money, the tithe box was the first to be filled, a testament to my commitment to putting God first and the reassurance of His presence in my financial matters.

It wasn't about the money. It was about putting God first and trusting Him with the rest. This principle was something God used to speak to my husband, John. Early in our relationship, God told him, "This is what I have for you; take care of her." This divine message affirmed our relationship and solidified John's commitment to our family, knowing God had brought us together for a purpose.

A Husband and a Van

In March 2010, life as a single mom homeschooling two boys was a mix of challenges, blessings, and endless to-dos. Although I was a mom of three, my daughter was already married and off starting her own life, which left me to pour my energy into my two boys. Our days were full of homeschooling lessons, trips to sports practices, and Boy Scout meetings. My faithful companion through it all was a 1992 Town & Country van that had seen better days. It got us where we needed to go, but just barely.

That old van had a mind of its own (my husband called it "demon-possessed")—the doors locked and unlocked randomly, the interior lights flickered like some kind of ghostly light show, and one of the passenger doors was barely hanging on. But the sliding door in the back was the worst; if I took a turn too quickly, it might fling itself open. I knew it was time for a replacement, so I'd saved $3,500 from my tax return, hoping that would be enough to get something more reliable. A customer from the restaurant where I worked owned a small car lot and said he'd help me find a van within my budget.

Little did I know my pastor and a few elders from our church were also working behind the scenes to find a way to help me get a new vehicle.

A retired missionary we had supported for years came to speak to our congregation one Sunday morning. He shared stories about the villages in Russia where he served, describing their needs and the struggle to keep people warm through brutal winters. As we prayed for his ministry, I saw a number—bright as neon, glowing red—hovering over his head. It was the first vision I'd ever had, and I couldn't ignore it. I had left my checkbook at home, so later that afternoon, I quickly slipped home to grab it before heading to a birthday party. I wrote a check for $3,000 and quietly handed it to my pastor.

Only a week later, a sudden freeze hit overnight, and my pipes burst, causing more stress. But once again, my church family stepped in. The men under sixty showed up at my house that Saturday and spent the whole day installing new plumbing in my attic. They came back on Sunday to finish the job. Their kindness demonstrated the true meaning of a church family and the support a spiritual community can provide.

To backtrack a bit, late the previous year, I had decided to stop trying to do everything on my own and had given my whole life—my dreams, goals, and even my hopes for a good man—over to God. Nothing I had tried alone had worked out how I'd hoped. I was a single mom of three, each of my children with a different father, and I'd been married twice, so I had finally been ready to hand everything over to God.

One day in December, an older gentleman from the restaurant where I worked, someone I only knew in conversations as I waited on him daily, asked if he could pass my number to his son. I smiled and said, "If your son wants my number, he can ask for it himself."

Now, his son, John, wasn't looking for a relationship. He'd been married for twenty-six years and wasn't keen on getting involved again. But his father was persistent, and one Saturday in early March, John agreed to join him for lunch. John asked for my number that day, but when he called, I was dealing with the pipes and told him I wasn't available right then.

A couple of weeks passed without a follow-up call. Then, one Tuesday evening, my phone rang while I had my boys at Boy Scouts. John explained that as he was clocking out, a small card fell from his sun visor right onto his lap with my number on it. He took it as a sign. We went on our first date that weekend.

I told him the story of donating $3,000 to the church as we talked. Not realizing I had already done it, John told me that if God had prompted me to give, I needed to follow through. That moment was a revelation for me—I knew then that this was the man God had chosen for me. His heart was aligned with mine in faith and trust in God's plan.

By May of that same year, I had an engagement ring on my finger and a new-to-me van in the driveway. John had sent me to look for a van, assuring me he would cover the cost regardless of where our relationship went. His generosity and commitment shone through even before we were officially engaged.

Fast-forward to 2024, and we celebrated our thirteenth wedding anniversary, fourteen years since that evening when I shared with him about my donation to the church's Faith Promise drive for missionaries. Listening to God's promptings brought me a new van and the husband He had planned for me, one who still cares for me excellently.

John's Health Journey

Over the years, John has faced more health challenges than we ever could have imagined. Although he wasn't diabetic, his feet seemed to bear the brunt of his troubles. It began with a small ulcer on his foot, which we thought would heal with a bit of care, but it didn't. That first ulcer kept him out of work for eight weeks. We spent those weeks at home together, streaming shows without a worry about how we'd manage, all thanks to the emergency fund we had put aside. God had provided, giving us peace even in that first trial.

The following year, a second ulcer appeared, this t me on his toe. It quickly became more serious as the infection spread into the bone. Despite all efforts to save it, John lost his toe to the infection and ended up missing another five weeks of work. It was a tough blow, but we held onto hope, praying this would end his foot troubles.

To relieve the pressure that kept causing these ulcers, John went through multiple surgeries, each one adding more screws to his feet in an attempt to stabilize them. It seemed like every time he returned to work, there was a new obstacle waiting. One of these ulcers happened during the height of the COVID shutdown. He was all set to have surgery, but just one day before the scheduled operation, the hospital shut down. The delay stretched on, and John was out of work for seven months between the extended shutdown and his recovery period after surgery.

During those months, John's company used government-provided COVID funds to pay him his regular forty-hour work week, allowing him to handle paperwork from home. Though it wasn't the overtime he was used to, it kept us financially steady through that long, uncertain season.

But his foot troubles were only part of the journey. One day, John was hit with severe stomach pain, so his primary care physician sent him to the hospital for tests. They ran a CT scan and noted slight signs of diverticulitis – inflammation in the large intestine – along with an enlarged kidney. Assuming the pain stemmed from the diverticulitis, they stopped investigating further. But just a week later, he was back in the hospital with the same intense pain. This time, they performed a scope and found an ulcer in his stomach. But the real concern was his enlarged kidney; further tests revealed a tumor. The only option was to remove the kidney to prevent the cancer from spreading. Once again, we found ourselves navigating surgery and recovery.

In 2023, they found a small growth in the space where his kidney had been. It was so tiny they didn't even biopsy it; it was safer to remove it.

Even during the process of writing for this book, God provided for us yet again. Real estate is one of the income streams my husband, John, and I have been building for his retirement. In late June of 2024, an opportunity promised a quick return, almost doubling our investment within a few months. I took the chance, and the investment paid off in early September—when we needed it most.

At the end of August, John developed another painful hole in his foot, putting him out of work once more. With the time off, he checked in on a few health concerns he had ignored. He made an appointment with his primary doctor, who quickly sent him to his heart specialist. They performed a heart catheterization and discovered a slight blockage. Due to its tricky placement, the doctor decided to treat it with medication, hoping that would be enough. But soon after, John failed a stress test, meaning more intervention was needed.

The doctor tried to place stents but couldn't get them in the right spot. He called in a heart surgeon, and just a week later, in the middle of September, John underwent a quadruple bypass. It turned out that the tiny blockage was where no stent could be placed and required two bypasses on each side.

Through it all, the real estate investment brought us peace. That return arrived just when we needed it, allowing us to stay steady through another season of uncertainty.

Through all these relentless trials, God's provision was constant. Each time John was forced to take off work, we were sustained. We had emergency funds to fall back on, disability payments, vacation time, and sick days that seemed to cover what we needed. Every step of the way, God showed us that He was in control, His provision reminding us that even in the darkest times, His light shines through. These blessings were a constant reassurance of His care, strengthening our faith and trust that we would be cared for no matter the circumstances.

A Journey of Online Businesses

My journey into the world of online business began in 1999. I found myself working in the main office of an internet shopping MLM company—a bustling hub of innovation and opportunity. When I eventually left, I didn't leave behind the connections I had made. Instead, I teamed up with a few colleagues from the company and dove headfirst into the world of Stay-at-Home Moms (SAHM), discovering vibrant online communities like Yahoo groups and forums. It was there that I immersed myself, teaching myself to hand-code HTML and build websites from scratch. Determined to find my niche, I used my newfound skills to run a small printing company, trained as a virtual assistant (VA), and eventually became a Christian Life Coach, helping others find direction in their lives.

I vividly remember those early days—the internet was still new and filled with endless opportunities to learn. I spent countless nights hunched over my computer, navigating coding tutorials and building websites. Each one I created, every new skill I mastered, filled me with a sense of accomplishment. But after a while, the details of web design wore on me. Even as technology evolved and design became more streamlined, I felt that I still hadn't found my true calling.

In 2005, life shifted yet again. Following another divorce, I started homeschooling my boys. My kids are all six years apart, so my daughter was already a junior in high school when I began homeschooling. This new chapter opened my eyes to new possibilities, and I was inspired to create a coaching program specifically for teens, helping them find ways to make money online. By 2010, I had begun integrating spiritual gifts into their entrepreneurial pursuits, hoping to provide a holistic approach to their growth. But life once again took a turn; marriage and family life became my priority, and I set my business aspirations aside.

In 2011, my oldest son, Dustin, decided to return to school to play football. To ensure he was ready, I had him take a placement test and an aptitude assessment. To my surprise, the results suggested he would make a great accountant. It seemed at odds with his athletic spirit and struggles with sleep apnea. However, a couple of years later, our church's spiritual gifts assessment and the DISC personality profile revealed that his strongest gifts were serving and giving, and his personality type was a Competent Specialist—traits well-suited to a career in accounting.

When my youngest son approached high school, I felt called to share my experiences and knowledge with other young people again. I decided to teach a career prep class at our homeschool co-op, and this class became the foundation for what I later named "Discerning My Calling." Through this program, I guided kids through various assessments, including personality, aptitude, and spiritual gifts. We looked at each result, weaving in their values, skills, and unique strengths to help them understand their purpose and potential.

Becoming a Kingdom Entrepreneur

By 2018, I had spent many years navigating the online business world, establishing my presence through LesaDale.com. As the new year approached, I felt a deep urge to seek God's guidance for the direction of my business. During this time of reflection and prayer, God gave me the word "Discover." It became clear that He wanted me to partner with Him more intentionally. I found a mentor, Shae Bynes, and her training at Kingdom Driven Entrepreneur.

As the beginning of 2019 rolled in, God told me that He had been trying to capture my attention for years, guiding me to intertwine spiritual gifts with personalities and business. This journey was not about my ambitions but about fulfilling His purpose. He said, "This is not about you; it's about me!" I knew I had to find a business name that worked for Him. Life Walk GPS was born with this understanding, culminating in years of learning, praying, and trusting God. The name says it all: walking with God through life, using our GPS (gifts, personality, and strength). It wasn't just a business; it was a ministry, a calling.

Irrevocable Success: Unlock Your Divine Purpose emerged to help others find and live out their God-given callings. The program is designed to guide individuals through discovering their unique purpose by focusing on their spiritual gifts, values, and personal strengths. It includes a comprehensive evaluation of one's current life satisfaction, making intentional space for God's presence, and cultivating a mindset rooted in spiritual and emotional abundance.

In the program, participants learn to align their daily actions with their divine purpose, building a foundation that supports their personal, professional, and spiritual growth. This alignment is about more than just discovering one's purpose—it's about living it out with intention and clarity, ensuring that every step is in harmony with God's plan. The journey also involves dreaming big dreams with God, exploring new possibilities, and understanding each individual's unique advantages as part of God's design.

Ultimately, the goal is to equip participants with the tools and mindset needed to achieve "irrevocable success"—a life of fulfillment, joy, and peace that can withstand any challenge because it is built on the unshakeable foundation of God's purpose.

"the gifts and calling of God are irrevocable." Romans 11:29

Looking back on my life, I see a tapestry woven with threads of God's provision and guidance. From budgeting with an antique vanity to becoming a Kingdom Entrepreneur, each experience has strengthened my confidence in His provision and allowed me to laugh at the future. This journey has led me to create *Irrevocable Success: Unlock Your Divine Purpose*, designed to help others discover and live out their God-given calling.

By trusting in God's faithfulness, we can move forward with joy and assurance, knowing He will continue to care for us. Proverbs 31:25 reminds us that when we are clothed with strength and dignity, we can laugh at the days to come, secure in the knowledge that God holds our future in His hands.

Contact Information:
Lesa Dale
Life Walk GPS, LLC
www.lesadale.com

She Designed a Life She Loved

Dawn E. Anderson

Trials, tragedies and triumphs.

A little background: I grew up in a pretty dysfunctional home. Alcoholism, lies by omission, and codependency were the norm. I believed that how I felt was not important.

Carrying that dysfunction into my adult life, I was searching for love. I knew God loved me... I remembered hearing about Jesus and at the age of four, believing that if someone could love me that much to die for me, I was going to trust that guy!

Wanting to feel loved is also most likely a big reason why I have eight children (six boys and two girls). Because it was one place I felt unconditionally loved. At least when they were young.

Yet, I always wanted my "happily ever after". There are many stories between then and now and I will fill you in on more of those in another book (I promise you will find them hard to believe). So, let's fast forward to my twenty-year marriage that ended several years ago.

First let me ask you a question. Have you ever found yourself being someone who inadvertently rescues (or tries to) rescue other people from their "circumstances". That was *me*! A huge sign of codependency and trying to feel whole is shown through trying to fix someone else. I wore the sign 'let me help you' with big flashing lights!

There were tons of red flags in that relationship and marriage. Not just the abuse in every area imaginable. More importantly things never changed… at least not for the better. It took some time before I realized I made a terrible Holy Spirit. I could not change, fix, or control anyone else. Nor should I want to. The bigger question became how much is *enough*? Sadly, my enough really didn't come until I realized that the impact on my children was getting worse and affecting them in traumatic ways. It is strange that I didn't value myself enough (yet) to think that the destruction of me wasn't enough to leave.

The last five years of my marriage, I was working in a company where personal development was key to my success. What I didn't know was it would be one of the keys in my eyes being opened to how toxic my environment was. One thing I can say for sure, is there is no timeline to change. It takes time. I remember being at a seminar with my husband at the time and hearing "You either have to change the people you are with or change the people you are with." Those words had a profound impact on me that day. Mostly because I had finally realized I couldn't change anyone but me. One other thing shared was that a healthy relationship should just flow; that 80% to 90% of the time it should be easy; and that the other percent of the time was where the raw, real, transparent feelings were exchanged. Not easy. But worth it. Because true intimacy is gained in those moments. Looking at my marriage… it was the exact opposite! Most of the time it was hard.

Dysfunction becomes normal. And the longer you live in 'CRAZY' the more normal it becomes. You don't even see it. Crazy becomes what you know. Have you ever heard the phrase "Doing the same thing over and over again, expecting a different result, is the definition of insanity." So essentially, I lived in insanity.

Several things happened that brought me closer to this realization. I remember one day when a friend of mine at the time stopped by my house while I was outside getting the mail. We walked around to the back of my lovely large home overlooking the golf course and sat down to chat. My husband then jumped out of the bushes asking me where the mail was. I immediately started explaining and apologizing to him for not bringing it to him right away. After grabbing the mail and walking away, my friend said, "Did you just apologize for getting the mail?" My initial response was one of trying to explain all the reasons I needed to bring it to him immediately. She asked me, "How old are you, and don't you ever receive mail?" At that moment my friend helped me see that I was being controlled by someone over the mail, which was certainly not healthy. That is one example of hundreds where I lived under the control of someone else. A keynote here is I accepted it and allowed it. I had no boundaries over what I allowed or accepted. Again, crazy.

Leaving

I planned to leave several times. When my fifth child was a baby, I told my husband I was going to leave him. His response was, "Go ahead. You will just be a two-time loser. No one else will want you with all these kids." Shame immediately kicked in. And I believed him. *'Who else would want me?'* I thought. *'No one',* was my answer. So, I stayed.

While pregnant with my eighth child I remember showing my mother and sister my bruises at Christmas time. They felt bad for me, yet didn't encourage me to leave. So again, I stayed.

Something I believe is very important to share right now is that I *chose it*! No, I didn't have the support I would have liked to make changes, yet that doesn't remove the responsibility. I obviously didn't believe I was worth having something better in my life, down to my subconscious. I did not believe I was *enough* either. I was questioning myself and wondering why no matter what I did it was not good enough. Maybe even for God. I will share more about that later.

Things I Learned

First of all, I learned I must take responsibility. Are you open to taking responsibility? That might be difficult. It might be there are many circumstances which have affected your life and that is why you are where you are. But get ready to throw this book right now, because I am here to tell you that you are exactly where you are… because YOU CHOSE TO BE HERE! I can hear many of you right now telling me, "But you don't know about what happened to me!" and you are right. I do not know exactly what has happened to you… just as you have no idea what shoes I have walked in or the challenges I experienced. But I can tell you that you can use the path you are on and use what you have been through as your excuse to stay STUCK where you are OR to catapult you to where you are going!

A friend of mine once said, "There is no difference between a rut and a grave, except for the depth of the hole!". That made total sense to me. It also scared me, because it made me wonder, *'If I am holding the shovel… am I digging my own grave?'*

Someone else said to me that I am where I am today, because I chose to be here. I really didn't know if I agreed with them at that moment. Inside, even if I hadn't taken responsibility in the past, I knew that there was some truth to that. I needed to decide where I was going, and maybe even *if* I was going!

Around that same time, I was having coffee with a friend, and I asked him, "Are you happy?"

His response was, "I'm comfortable" with a smile on his face.

I think that answer was one he had not only given before, but one that let him stay exactly where he was for a very long time.

I knew at that moment that the only way my life was going to change was if I was willing to become UNCOMFORTABLE!

That's when I realized I needed a head and heart alignment knowing what I believed in my head and getting my heart (how I felt) to align. I knew what the Bible says. I believed God's promises in my head. Yet, I needed my heart to fully grasp it.

So, what happened? You might be wondering: how did I finally get up the courage to leave?

It took some more *years;* a lot more encounters with people God put in my life to continue to open my eyes. I asserted more boundaries which definitely caused more conflict. Sadly, it also took more abuse (as it continued to worsen).

The final straws were around the sexual abuse of myself and one of my children. It seems slightly pathetic even just writing that out. However, I believe all of it has served a divine purpose in me living out the purpose God has for me. Including sharing with you. To know that someone else understands your pain and can also stand up and remind you that we can use our tragedies to become our biggest triumphs can help us have the strength to change. We can laugh at the future because He helped us get through our past. And our past never has to be indicative of our future.

Walking Away

So often we try and figure out "how" things will work out, especially when we don't see a plausible way. Yet one thing I have learned is that truly trusting in God is not knowing the "how", only believing the why. I never imagined how it would or could work out for me to leave.

Honestly, one day I just snapped. I had had enough, and it didn't even seem like it was a 'big deal', looking back at all the horrific things I experienced over the years. It was, however, exactly what I needed. My breaking point.

The evening before I left my marriage, when I got home from work, I knew an argument was ensuing from the moment I came through the door. I went into one of the kids' rooms to sleep and locked the door. He continued to yell, and I informed him I was not going to talk to him. He decided to kick the door down. It wasn't the first time he broke a door. At that point I told him it didn't matter how many doors he kicked down, I was not having a conversation. He left the room. The next morning, I went to get my car keys to pick up my daughter's from a sleepover they had the night before so we could go to church.

When I went to get my keys from where they were always hung, they weren't there. I asked my husband where my keys were. He proceeded to tell me. "You don't have a car." Thinking he was joking, I asked for them again. I got the same response. THAT WAS IT.... THAT WAS THE MOMENT. I said, "When I met you, I had a car, and you didn't. When I met you, I had a home, and you didn't. I had everything, and you had nothing, and now you are going to tell me I don't have a car?" Right then, I picked up the phone, called a friend and said, "I need a ride." I made a decision that day, in that moment, and I knew I was never going back.

I was prepared for him to try and find my price point (meaning how he could buy me back). Yet my decision was made. So even though he brought me my car after a couple of days and a checkbook with some money in it (up to that point we had no joint funds or credit cards, he controlled the money too), I knew I had no price. I laugh about it now because even when he brought me the checkbook, he told me where I was allowed to spend it. I just shook my head. He still wanted control. There was no amount of money worth the price of freedom.

You can always start again. Staying stuck is not an option. Moving forward is.

As a mom of eight I wondered if I could really do it alone. Even with God's help, the task of providing financially was my biggest hurdle.

One thing is for certain: God doesn't change people that do not want to be changed.

The idea of "helping people" or rather "rescuing someone" from themselves and their circumstances stems from codependency and what I learned growing up in a very dysfunctional alcoholic home. Funny how we can become quick to rescue someone else and yet never rescue ourselves. I realized that no one was going to come along on a white horse and rescue me. God gave me the horse, and I needed to jump on and ride away.

Thoughts Are Things

Have you ever heard the phrase, "What you think about expands"? It is so true. So, if all I do is think about the negative, then the negative will expand. Conversely, that same principle is true when thinking about positive things.

We become conditioned to think about why something won't work versus why it will. The trend tends to be negative and so we just jump on that band wagon, and we blend right in.

Imagine if you saw life from the perspective of how you want it to look, instead of how you don't?

God's timeline - even when I had *no idea* how was when trusting Him came in. I learned to thank Him for the vision He gave me of how it will be, and then be grateful for it (as if it already had).

Two Voices

As my journey continued, I knew I must continue to seek out what my belief systems really were and where they originated. After one-on-one counseling for four years, reading numerous books, attending seminars, listening to audios and watching numerous videos, I knew that I wanted to have someone else who could help me identify the "things between my ears" that lurked about and were assisting me in the wrong direction. At that point I hired a "coach". For the first time money was not the object or the hurdle because I knew that in order for things to change, I had to figure it out and I had to change. As I was debriefing "my week" to my coach, she asked me, "Why do you talk to yourself the way you do?"

At first, I didn't even realize it. Then I listened to myself. It was a harsh, mean, critical, judgmental, perfectionist voice. One that demanded instantaneous action to correct whatever it was that wasn't exactly how it should be. That voice certainly didn't motivate me (which is what the purpose of the voice was supposed to be) and instead of moving me into action, I felt debilitated and overwhelmed. It was a place where I wanted to do nothing (so that I didn't do anything else wrong). This critical voice was the one that said things like, "Well if you just got your butt out of bed an hour earlier than your workout could be finished before anyone else is even up!" There was a voice that said, "Yeah, well, you said that you were going to accomplish that before, and it still isn't done yet!"

The sound of that voice had lingered in my head since childhood. The voice that said I was never good enough, and only if I worked really hard, for a very long time, then maybe someone would realize my heart.

My true and kind intention was that I wanted to be good, but I just made mistakes. It was not on purpose. Not to hurt anyone. I thought, '*I must be so self-centered.*' (Because I was told so often by my ex and yet I couldn't see it.) I questioned it when I knew I sacrificed so much for others. How was I not putting others first? Really, was that how everyone else felt?

Those lies were engrained in me by the narcissists in my life. They perpetuated my thought patterns and kept me from trusting. I lived "on guard" almost like a detective always watching for clues as to how the people around me wanted to fool me and create pain. So, to protect myself, I had a voice whose only purpose was to keep me in check and make sure I stayed on task. The only problem was that voice didn't work. It didn't keep me on task. Instead, it stopped me dead in my tracks.

It was then my coach said, "What would the kind, gentle voice say to you?" It was time to send that negative, yucky voice away on a permanent vacation.

How about that positive voice? One where the intention was good? Where expectations were few? A voice that said, "People do not want to hurt you." A voice that allowed me to trust. Not that I was trusting everyone else; I learned I could trust *myself* and truly trust *God*. I could be my own best friend. It was a place where I could be true to myself.

How come when it comes to us, the whole person, mind, body and spirit, we seldom are willing to put the time or the money into developing into all that we were destined to become? Education as we know it (grade school, high school, college) only teaches us a limited number of things. The rest comes from where? For most of us, only the immediate influences of the people we surround ourselves with. How can you change where you are stuck if you don't know how? *You don't know what you don't know*!

The exciting thing is that your past does not equal your future. And it doesn't even equal your present because right now, just from the impact of these words, life cannot be exactly the same. You see, now you know!

"Know what?" you might be saying.

You know more than you did before you started reading this, and most importantly, you now know *you are responsible*! Isn't it incredible that you are not even the same person you were ten minutes ago?

Recognizing the old story became very important for me. It was so life changing for me when I realized I was the writer with the pen, and I could rewrite my past by assigning a new meaning to everything I had experienced so far. I remembered the power of my words and that the sound of my own voice was the most powerful voice there is.

So I paid attention to the verbiage I used, and if I said something that wasn't empowering, I changed it and said it again using a better choice of words. For instance, instead of saying, "I could never do that," I rephrased it to, "in the past I wouldn't have believed I could do that, now I am getting stronger every day. So that's easy. I can do that too!"

I also began valuing myself and my emotions. If I felt icky inside from a circumstance or words that someone else said, I would look deeper and ask myself, "Where is this really coming from?"

Here is a life example.

I was riding in the car with a friend. When I started talking about something that made him uncomfortable, he said, "I'm not talking about this anymore."

I looked out the window and tears started falling down my face. I stopped and thought, *'Where is this pain coming from?'* God revealed to me in that moment a time when I was a teenager when I was given some shocking and surprising news.

I was a senior in high school and right after a fire drill, a girl I had known for years came up to me and said, "Hey, Dawn, your dad might be my dad!"

My first thought was she must have been doing drugs during that fire drill. However, she then proceeded to tell me that she was with another one of our friends outside, and they saw a work truck go by. She had said to our mutual friend, "My dad might be driving that truck!"

Our friend said, "What? That's Dawn's dad's company."

As she shared that story and then proceeded to name my relatives, I started to cry. Actually, we both did. We were the same age and only one month apart.

We went and called "our" grandmother who came and got us and proceeded to share that indeed my dad was her dad.

Needless to say, I was devastated and wasn't thinking highly of my father at that time. When my grandmother dropped me off at home, my mother was there to greet me. My mother proceeded to tell me, "You know this is really hard for your father, so it really would be good if you just didn't say anything."

The message I received out of that. "Your feelings don't matter, and I don't want to hear them."

I continued to live by that code: believing that how I felt didn't matter. So, there I was in that car and at that moment I was able to realize that I was experiencing those same feelings and emotions from when I was a teenager. Once I was able to identify that, I decided to share it with the other person. I simply said that even if they didn't want to talk about it, my feelings were important, and I desired to feel heard and my feelings to be acknowledged. It was uncomfortable for sure, yet it was a huge place of growth for me.

A Leap Forward

You know those times when you think you have a plan, and it will look or go a certain way? Then all of a sudden you are pushed to move forward. That's one of the things which happened next. My divorce had been final for a while. Due to the abuse, I was granted sole legal and physical custody of all the minor children. This meant I could move anywhere. At that time, our home was in Minnesota. However, I knew I was going to move to the ocean. I literally picked out the place on a map. I had never been, and didn't know a soul who lived there either. I told everyone we were moving to the beach.

For two years I watched the weather there every day. I also read a card I had written a few years before out loud. It said, "I just took my sandals off at the bottom of the steps, feeling the warm sand between my toes. The sun is shining, and the ocean waves are crashing. I look up and see my new home and say, 'I did it!'" So that was the plan.

I was back living in the house with my children waiting for the house to sell. My ex-husband was extremely uncooperative in the process. Not unusual. He decided the kids and I were the reason the house wasn't selling, so he went to court and convinced the judge he needed to be in charge of selling the house and we needed to get out. My plan was that the house would sell so I would have more money to put down on the house I planned to purchase on the beach.

Well, the judge sided with him and literally gave us two weeks to move. That meant we had to empty the 4,000 sq ft home and leave within fourteen days. At that point I was not going to move twice or move into an apartment in that small town in Minnesota.

So the purge began. I gave away more than I could sell in that short period of time and threw the rest away. I ordered a small moving truck with a flatbed for my car. I wouldn't be taking any furniture with me (honestly, I didn't want the memories anyway). I packed up as much of my kitchen (I love to cook) and had to choose carefully as there wasn't a lot of room. There were so many decisions to make in that short period of time. We kept clothes that were pertinent to the warmer weather, photos and some memorabilia. Those fourteen days went by very quickly and the stress was, well, let's just say over the top. Not to mention a couple of days before we were leaving, I was told the home we thought we would move into on the island was no longer going to work out due to damage to the property. That meant when we got there we would have nowhere to live and so I needed to figure that out too!

Two days later we shut the door on the moving truck, loaded my car onto the flatbed behind it, climbed into the truck and started our drive from Minnesota to North Carolina, where I have now lived for over eleven years. Finding a new place to live on the island once we got there was another adventure, and it took several days (while we lived in a hotel with the moving truck in the parking lot.) *Here* is the cool part; when I went to look at the new possibility of a home on the island (through a series of events and people God totally put together), I walked in and immediately knew it was the right place. I could even see the ocean from our balcony. After unpacking the truck, we walked out onto the beach and guess what?

I just took my sandals off at the bottom of the steps, feeling the warm sand between my toes. The sun was shining, and the ocean waves were crashing. I looked up and saw my new home and said, 'I did it!'

But the coolest part was I didn't even realize it was happening just the way I had said it out loud all that time. It hit me afterwards. The powerful ways our subconscious mind works.

Forgiveness

There is power in forgiveness. I realized that in order to move forward and heal from my past, forgiveness was key. Not for someone else but for me. I understood I needed to forgive everyone, whether I felt justified in my anger or not. I also realized that often forgiveness comes in stages, like peeling away at something.

There were people I thought I had forgiven and then found I had another layer of bitterness or hurt stored up that needed to be released. I also learned that I didn't have to have the strength to forgive on my own. Instead, I could envision God's forgiveness towards me and then let that flow from Him through me. It was not by my strength but His.

Something I had yet to realize was that the one big person I still needed to forgive was *me.* That was honestly the toughest (a work in progress). Yet it has certainly been the most freeing.

And one way I was truly able to grasp this forgiveness was through the following revelation.

Another Revelation

After understanding forgiveness of others and how essential it was. There was a piece of forgiveness I was yet to realize.

I met with an incredible woman who helped me look closer at my relationship with God. Not just the Father, but the Trinity. She asked me who I felt closest to and who seemed farther away.

I shared that I felt the farthest from God the Father.

She asked why.

I shared that I felt like He just looked at me from heaven shaking His head, wondering why it took me so long to learn my lessons. I felt like I was always on the witness stand and He was the judge ready to pass judgement on me.
She asked me about my earthly father that raised me.

I gleaned a lot of how I looked at my heavenly Father from that earthly relationship. I felt as though I needed to be perfect to be loved.

I then imagined myself entering the throne room, where my Father actually called me in to sit next to Him. I imagined Him only showing me compassion and unconditional love. I put my head in His lap, and He stroked my head with nothing but grace, mercy and understanding. That is when I realized the person I had yet to forgive was myself.

This shifted my relationship with God. I no longer felt like I was living under the guise of the expectation that somehow, I was to be perfect. I felt His forgiveness and a healing took place. I experienced a feeling of His overwhelming love for me. There is nothing God loves more than me. (Or YOU).

This has been a powerful journey of learning who God created me to be and the purpose He put within me. I find the blessing in every lesson and challenge.

Come celebrate the journey with me. You are not alone.

Remember: Life is a journey not a destination. It is a process. Stay in the moment! You can do it!

Contact Information:
Dawn Anderson
Bestselling Author. Speaker. Realtor. Success Coach.
www.DawnAndersonCoaching.com

Seasons of Hope

Jill Albanys

*An excellent woman [one who is spiritual, capable, intelligent, and virtuous]...
Strength and dignity are her clothing, and her position is strong and secure;
she smiles at the future [knowing that she and her family are prepared].
Proverbs 31:10, 25 AMP*

Summer has come and gone; the leaves have now fallen to cover the earth with a quilted blanket of colors slowly fading in decay. Winter with its chilling winds bring the hibernation of everything that bears fruit causing all to sleep as harvest is now past.

Seasons bring change and change can bring joy or sorrow, laughter or tears.

Scripture tells us that there is an appointed time for everything.

What season are you in?
What season are you facing?
Is your heart steady as you see what is on the horizon?
Do you know that the Lord will take care of you?

The woman in Proverbs 31 is a great example of how to prepare oneself to be unmoved by life's forecasts and even have a source of joy when considering the long months of waiting. Fridged winds seem to touch the soul as flakes of winter come to cover all sign of tender earth, stilling the sternest of herbs as all sounds of summer are quieted by the cold. It seems winter demands another level of strength; it is a time of surviving with things stored up from the previous season, a time of struggle and even isolation.

Winters in the Northwoods, Michigan, are beautiful yet treacherous. It is a season that requires awareness, forethought and purpose to endure. By the end of fall, one will see stacks of firewood growing each day as signs of summer fun are packed and stored away for another time to come.

This to me represents the seasons of life and how there are times of growth, times of harvest, times of laughter, times of heartache, yet in all things and in all seasons of life, we trust the Lord.

The Proverbs 31 woman was prepared. Her heart and mind were settled as she served the Lord first and foremost in all things. She took her faith in God into all that she did for her family, and she was diligent to do the necessary things to get ready for the seasons that could bring hardship.

Jeremiah 17:7 Blessed is the man that trusteth in the Lord, and **whose hope** the Lord is.

I have found it easy to trust God in seasons of peace and joy. It is the season of hardship and trial that tries the faith of the most avid believer and brings a looming fear, which each of us may feel in these times.

Life will bring things that cause hearts to skip a beat as we hold our breath to await the pending outcome, something I experienced recently.

The day had started with sunshine and a wonderful Sunday service. My mother was visiting, and we'd just shared a meal together. Everything seemed well, the day unfolding like so many Sundays before it. And then it happened—the season changed.

The phone rang, and the voice on the other end bore a cry of mourning: my younger brother was dead. I felt life drain from me as I screamed out in denial. *How could this be?*

Within minutes, we were in my vehicle, racing across town. I could hear my mother praying repeatedly, calling on the God of heaven and earth, *"He is not dead; he is not dead!"* Her cries seemed to nudge me forward in faith, urging me to pray, to believe, to hold on to hope for my brother. We needed a miracle.

Ten minutes later, we rushed into my brother's home to find him lying on the floor, surrounded by firemen and rescue workers. His eyes were fixed, his body lifeless, as one machine forced his chest up and down, and another sent air into his lungs.

This was the moment when faith itself became the ground I stood on. I refused to accept what I was seeing and looked upon his body with eyes of hope. All I knew was that if Jesus could call Lazarus from the dead, then we, as children of God, could call back my brother. So, I began calling out his name, and my mother made her way to pray over him.

It felt like time stood still as we battled death, calling life to prevail, yet it was only moments after my mother prayed, it happened. A whispered voice broke through the stillness: *"He took a breath."* The woman stationed at his head saw him breathe on his own and checked for a pulse in his neck. She nodded, saying, *"He is alive."*

My brother had been dead for twenty minutes, and everyone in the room, believer and unbeliever alike, witnessed the real, miraculous power of resurrection. The same power that raised Jesus from the grave raised my brother back to life.

The battle continued over the next few days as we awaited each doctor's report. We fasted and prayed, standing and declaring day after day, even as one specialist said he was brain dead and another later declared brain damage. But we watched as my brother defied every report, reaching the point where he could return home just weeks after he'd collapsed.

This was a time of deep sorrow for our family, a time of waiting, a time of trouble. Our hearts broke moment by moment as we prayerfully anticipated each new day. Yet despite the shadows that loomed, every sunrise brought new hope, as we watched mercy unfold and life continue. Our trial of heart and soul turned into joy as the spark of life returned to my brother's eyes and laughter once again filled our beings. My brother opened his eyes, and God said, "He will live."

Seasons.
There is a season for everything. (Ecclesiastes 3)
Just as God created seasons in the world, so there are also different seasons in our lives.
Some seasons will be filled with laughter, others with tears.
Some seasons will be for resting, others for much labor.
There are seasons when we will walk through the valley of the shadow of death, and seasons when we see our loved ones raised back to life.
But in every season, we will trust the Lord. In every season we know that He is in control.

The Proverbs 31 character shows us that we, as women who fear the Lord, have nothing to fear in this life. We know and believe that God will carry us through everything and will use all things for our good.

As we consider *She Laughs at the Future*, the faith we have in our Heavenly Father supplies us with a source of peace and joy in whatever the seasons may bring.

So many lessons were learned as we walked the valley with my brother but one stands out the brightest.

Today is the day of salvation. Today is the day we have with our loved ones who surround us. Today is the day we have to grow closer to the Lord and build up our faith in Him.

Tomorrow is in the womb of time to be woven together in the tapestry of life and skillfully designed in the Master's hand. We don't need to worry. He will take care of His children.

Seasons come and seasons go.

Spring time is one of my favorite times of year as we say good-bye to the snow-covered earth with the blankets of white and skies of grey. I love to put winter to rest as we welcome with open arms the season of warmth that rushes in with its companions of promise and growth.

Whatever season you are in, whatever it is that you may be facing today, it will one day pass to become a declaration and testimonial of God's faithfulness in all things. We have a promise that He will make all things new.

Romans 15:13, May the God of hope fill you with all joy and peace as you trust in him, so that you may overflow with hope by the power of the Holy Spirit.

Psalm 18:1, "I love you, Lord, my strength. The Lord is my rock, my fortress, and my deliverer; my God is my rock, in whom I take refuge, my shield and the horn of my salvation, my stronghold."

Isaiah 26:4 AMP, "Trust [confidently] in the Lord forever [He is your fortress, your shield, your banner], For the Lord God is an everlasting Rock [the Rock of Ages].

We can laugh in the rain and rejoice in the pain because we have hope, and hope endures.

As daughters of the King, we can rest in God's power, purpose and provision. No matter what we face we can see God working in the midst of every circumstance.

As children of God, we can laugh when facing the future because our heart is set on Him and we know He is a good-good father. He loves us, oh how He loves us....

I will leave you with this famous passage of scripture as you lift your eyes to the maker of heaven and earth. He will keep you through every season that life brings your way; you are never alone. Let your heart be established in faith as you tilt your head back, receive the joy of the Lord, and laugh without worry or fear of the future.

A Time for Everything

1 There is a season (a time appointed) for everything and a time for every delight *and* event *or* purpose under heaven—
2 A time to be born and a time to die;
A time to plant and a time to uproot what is planted.
3 A time to kill and a time to heal; A time to tear down and a time to build up.

4 A time to weep and a time to laugh; A time to mourn and a time to dance.

5 A time to throw away stones and a time to gather stones; A time to embrace and a time to refrain from embracing.

6 A time to search and a time to give up as lost; A time to keep and a time to throw away.

7 A time to tear apart and a time to sew together; A time to keep silent and a time to speak.

8 A time to love and a time to hate; A time for war and a time for peace.

Contact Information:

Jill Albanys

Author. Speaker. Successful Entrepreneur, Business, and Life Coach.

www.jillalbanys.com

Facebook: facebook.com/jill.albanys

Appendix A
About the Authors

In order of appearance:

Katelyn Silva

Katelyn Silva is the 6x international bestselling author of thirteen books, some under a pen name. She is a God-fearing devoted wife and home-schooling mother of four. She is the founder of We Write Books, Coffee Date with Jesus, and is the host of the 1 Minute Writing Tip podcast. She works with Holy Spirit-led women to get clarity on their book idea, confidently write and publish a bestseller, and use it as a tool for impact, authority, and accomplishing their God-given purpose. She believes every person has a unique story worth telling and that your book can change a life. Learn more at www.wewritebooks.com.

Melissa Eiserer

Melissa Eiserer BSE, MS, Founder and CEO of Melissa Eiserer Career Coaching and Consulting, is a sought-after career and school counselor with 30+ years of experience specializing in personal career coaching, consulting, job preparation, and professional training. She is a faith-based career coach, speaker, and professional, who works with all students and homeschool families to explore career options beyond high school. She guides students to find their best career pathway, minimize higher education debt, and step into a successful future by determining who they want to be and what that might look like. Learn more by connecting on Facebook: www.facebook.com/melissa.eiserer.

Helen Corban

Helen of Reach Potential is an expert in business, time management, and leadership, with nearly 30 years of experience helping professionals accelerate growth and achieve sustainable success. Her work spans industries including government, education, corporate sectors, SMEs, and not-for-profit organizations. Helen's strategic, results-driven approach empowers individuals to unlock their potential and thrive, both professionally and personally. Based in New Zealand, she has worked globally, including in England, Japan, the Pacific Islands, and the USA. Helen is a dedicated mother of two, a long-standing member of LIFE Central in Auckland, and played a pivotal role in launching Catalyst Church in 2023. Learn more at www.reachpotential.co.nz.

Patty Schaad

Patty is a joyful entrepreneur, passionate puppy lover, and a woman on a mission to share the love of Jesus through her faith. As the owner of Patty's Pawsitive Services, a Christian pet-sitting business, she brings God's love and care to furry friends near and far. With a heart full of faith and a deep love for animals, she provides trusted pet-sitting services that ensure pets are happy, safe, and cherished. Learn more by connecting on Facebook at: www.facebook.com/pattyspawsitivity.

Audrey Ostoyic

Audrey Ostoyic is a serial entrepreneur with over two decades of experience in SEO and has walked a faith journey marked by both trials and triumphs. A lifelong Christian, Audrey has faced seasons of doubt, fear, and deep pain, especially after losing her mother to cancer—a loss that led her down a dark path where hope felt distant. Yet, Audrey's story is one of redemption and resilience, as she has come to embrace the truth that nothing enters her life without first passing through the loving hands of God. She lives with the assurance that all things are for her good and His glory. Learn more at www.audreyostoyic.com.

Shontal LeJune

Shontal LeJune is an Integrative Nutrition Health Coach, certified by the Institute of Integrative Nutrition. Her approach came through her own experience overcoming undiagnosed health issues post-pregnancy, which led to complete transformation through holistic learning and practices. She now helps others also experience health and life transformation through positive, holistic practices and changes. Learn more at www.SunshineLiving.com.

Renee Kelley

Renee Kelley is an author, speaker, minister, life coach, and realtor. Renee loves inspiring others to greatness. Renee is very passionate about helping others reach their dreams."

Learn more by connecting on Facebook at: www.facebook.com/renee.kelley.5.

Karen Powers

Karen Powers is a mom, wife, full-time special education teacher, Integrative Nutrition Health Coach, and a published author who is dedicated to guiding individuals to live healthier, happier lives through sustainable lifestyle changes. With a degree in education and years of experience as a teacher, she has the skills to guide, motivate and inspire others.

Learn more at www.simplywholeistic.com.

Denise LeDoux Leiato

Denise Leiato is a retired teacher and cancer survivor who has a passion to share her story of healing with others. Although she has faced many challenges in life, she desires to declare the goodness of God and His faithfulness, She wants to give hope to the hopeless and discouraged, for "God is not a respecter of persons." Learn more by connecting on

Facebook at www.facebook.com/denise.leiato.

DeAnna Cavenah

DeAnna Cavenah is a wife, mom, grandmother, Speaker, author of *Not Defined by the Struggle*, a worship pastor and songwriter, and, most importantly, a lover of Jesus. She graduated in 1989 from Delta School of Business in Lake Charles, LA with a Business Degree in Word Processing Technology. She pursued her career as an Office Manager for many years before she ventured out to become a Real Estate Agent and later became the owner of her own business, The Treasure Chest. DeAnna co-pastors Full Life Assembly of God in Dequincy, Louisiana, alongside her husband Greg. Learn more at www.dequincyfulllife.com

Victoria Bennett

Victoria Bennett is the owner of *Booth #5 – Vintage and Grace* where she displays her various crafts and antiques, with inspiration from her walk with the Holy Spirit. She is passionate about God and sharing hope and encouragement and faith with others through her creative gifts.

Learn more at: facebook.com/groups/1103640528152733.

Zeni Pradel

Zeni is a gifted designer and lover of God. She expresses her faith through designs of various items to help you wear your faith. Learn more at: https://zenidesignedco.etsy.com.

Lesa Dale

Lesa Dale, a lover of the Lord and plain ol' coffee, founded Life Walk GPS, LLC. As a Kingdom Purpose & Alignment Guide, speaker, and author trained in Spiritual Gifts and DISC profiling, she helps Christians move from uncertainty to confidence by discovering God's unique purpose for their lives. Using assessments of gifts, personalities, and strengths, Lesa equips her clients to make life decisions that align with God's plan, allowing them to thrive, become a light to the world doing what lights them up, and create a legacy of abundance. Learn more at www.lesadale.com.

Dawn Anderson

Dawn Anderson is a powerhouse who has walked through much adversity and come out a conqueror. She is a single mom of eight, a bestselling author, a realtor, a highly sought-after speaker, and a success coach. Dawn has spoken to thousands and is passionate about encouraging and empowering others to pursue their passion and live life by design. She teaches others how to "start from within" to make lasting changes. Learn more at: www.DawnAndersonCoaching.com.

Jill Albanys

With years of real estate sales experience and personal business success, Jill Albanys is passionate about helping women in their entrepreneurial journeys by providing the necessary elements of community and support which she has found to be the lifeblood of motivation and inspiration in every successful business. After all, no one wants to feel alone! Jill is passionate about serving others from a platform of faith and real encouragement and helping them understand God's desire is *for* them in their life and business. She provides the tools to help you achieve your desired level of success. Jill's motto is "I am not LIVING unless I AM GIVING!" Learn more and connect with Jill at www.jillalbanys.com or on Facebook at facebook.com/jill.albanys.

Thank You

Thank you so much for reading. We hope you have been inspired and encouraged by these stories. If you were touched, would you share your honest review on the book page? It will help us reach more readers and impact more lives.

Then, will you also share with someone you know?

We appreciate you!